December 2–6, 2012
Boston, Massachusetts

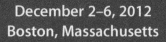

**Association for
Computing Machinery**

Advancing Computing as a Science & Profession

HILT'12

Proceedings of the ACM Conference on
High Integrity Language Technology

Sponsored by:
ACM SIGAda

In cooperation with:
**ACM SIGAPP, ACM SIGBED, ACM SIGCAS, ACM SIGCSE,
ACM SIGPLAN, and Ada-Europe**

**Association for
Computing Machinery**

Advancing Computing as a Science & Profession

ISBN: 978-1-4503-1505-0

Additional copies may be ordered prepaid from:

ACM Order Department
PO Box 30777
New York, NY 10087-0777, USA

Phone: 1-800-342-6626 (USA and Canada)
+1-212-626-0500 (Global)
Fax: +1-212-944-1318
E-mail: acmhelp@acm.org
Hours of Operation: 8:30 am – 4:30 pm ET

ACM Order Number: 825120

Printed in the USA

Welcome to ACM SIGAda's Annual International Conference High Integrity Language Technology – HILT 2012

Welcome to Boston and to HILT 2012, this year's annual international conference of the ACM Special Interest Group on the Ada Programming Language (SIGAda).

HILT 2012 features a top-quality technical program focused on the issues associated with **high integrity software** – where a failure could cause loss of human life or have other unacceptable consequences – and on the solutions provided by **language technology**. "Language technology" here encompasses not only programming languages but also languages for expressing specifications, program properties, domain models, and other attributes of the software or the overall system.

HILT 2012 consists of two days of tutorials, and three days of conference sessions. The **tutorials** cover a wide range of topics: designing for multitasking and multicore environments; leading-edge Ada verification technologies; contract-based programming and object-oriented programming in Ada 2012; safety of embedded software; Microsoft Research's Dafny automatic program verifier; Service-Oriented Architecture; and safety-critical Java.

The conference program includes **keynote presentations** from internationally recognized experts:

- **Kathleen Fisher** (DARPA Information Innovation Office), on High-Assurance Cyber Military Systems (HACMS) / High-Assurance Vehicles;
- **Nancy Leveson** (MIT), on Challenges for Safety-Critical Software;
- **Barbara Liskov** (MIT), on Programming the Turing Machine;
- **Greg Morrisett** (Harvard Univ.), on Hardening Legacy C/C++ Code; and
- **Guy L. Steele, Jr.** (Oracle Labs), on Programming Language Life Cycles.

HILT 2012 **conference sessions** deal with a range of topics associated with **safe, secure and reliable software**: analyzing and proving programs (program verification at compile time, advancing compilation technology); security and safety; real-time systems; and designing and implementing languages (compiler certification issues). You will learn the latest developments in software verification technologies, and hear industrial presentations from practitioners. The accompanying **exhibits** will give you the opportunity to meet vendors and find out about their latest offerings. Vendors include AdaCore (Platinum Level); Ellidiss, LDRA, Microsoft Research, and TASC (Silver Level); and MathWorks (Basic Level).

At HILT 2012 you will learn about both the challenges confronting high integrity software and the solutions available to address them. Perhaps just as important are the social interactions that you get at a live conference: the chance to meet and talk with researchers and practitioners in industry, academia, and government, to ask them questions, and to explain your own work and interests. These renewed and new associations can be as valuable as the technical program at professional conferences, and their benefits will continue to reward you well after you return home.

HILT 2012 Conference Chair

Ben Brosgol
AdaCore

HILT 2012 Program Co-Chairs

Jeff Boleng
Software Engineering Institute

S. Tucker Taft
AdaCore

Table of Contents

Keynote Address

Session 3: Languages and Security

Session 4: Languages and Safety – Track 1 Industrial Session on Safety

Session 5: Languages and Safety – Track 2 Real Time Systems

Keynote Address

Session 6: Compiler Certification Issues

Author Index

SIGAda HILT 2012 Conference Organization

Conference Chair:	Ben Brosgol *(AdaCore)*
Program Co-Chairs:	Jeff Boleng *(The Software Engineering Institute)*
	Tucker Taft *(AdaCore)*
Exhibits and Sponsorships Chair:	Alok Srivastava *(TASC, Inc.)*
Proceedings Chair:	Jeff Boleng *(The Software Engineering Institute)*
Local Arrangements Chair:	Ben Brosgol *(AdaCore)*
Workshops Chair:	John W. McCormick *(University of Northern Iowa)*
Publicity Chair:	Greg Gicca *(AdaCore)*
Treasurer:	Ricky E. Sward *(The MITRE Corporation)*
Registration Chair:	Michael Feldman *(George Washington Univ., retired)*
Tutorials Chair:	John W. McCormick *(University of Northern Iowa)*
Academic Community Liaison:	Michael Feldman *(George Washington Univ., retired)*
Webmaster:	Clyde Roby *(Institute for Defense Analyses)*
Logo Designer:	Weston Pan *(Raytheon Space and Airborne Systems)*
SIGAda Chair:	Ricky E. Sward *(The MITRE Corporation)*
SIGAda Vice Chair for Meetings and Conferences:	Alok Srivastava *(TASC, Inc.)*
SIGAda International Representative:	Dirk Craeynest *(K. U. Leuven, Belgium)*
Program Committee:	Jeff Boleng *(The Software Engineering Institute)*
	Tucker Taft *(AdaCore)*
	Jonathan Aldrich *(Carnegie-Mellon University)*
	Howard Ausden *(Lockheed Martin Corporation)*
	Lennart Beringer *(Princeton University)*
	Rod Chapman *(Altran-Praxis)*
	David Hardin *(Rockwell Collins, Inc.)*
	John Hatcliff *(Kansas State University)*
	Matt Heaney *(Google, Inc.)*
	James Hunt *(aicas)*
	John Knight *(University of Virginia)*
	Jim Larus *(Microsoft Corporation)*
	Kelvin Nilsen *(Atego, Inc.)*
	Erhard Ploedereder *(University of Stuttgart)*
	Jean-Pierre Rosen *(Adalog)*
	Joe Stoy *(Bluespec, Inc.)*
	Eric Van Wyk *(University of Minnesota)*
	Mitchell Wand *(Northeastern University)*

HILT 2012 Sponsor & Supporters

Sponsor:

In cooperation with:

HILT'12 Tutorial Overview
Design of Multitask Software:
The Entity-Life Modeling Approach

Bo I. Sandén
Colorado Technical University
4405 N. Chestnut Street
Colorado Springs, CO 80907
(719) 531-9045
bsanden@acm.org

ABSTRACT

The tutorial introduces entity-life modeling (ELM), a design approach for multitask, reactive software. It is not a multistep method but rather an extension of object orientation into the time dimension: The central idea is that the task architecture should reflect concurrency that exists in the problem. The tutorial uses Ada terminology and is illustrated with multiple Ada examples.

Categories and Subject Descriptors

D.2.2 [**Software Engineering**]: Design Tools and Techniques

General Terms

Design

Keywords

multitasking, entity-life modeling, multiprocessors, event threads, resource sharing, design of multitask software, multithreading, task architecture, reactive systems

1. INTRODUCTION

The tutorial introduces entity-life modeling (ELM). It is a design approach for multitask, *reactive* software, that is software that responds to events in the environment as they occur. It is not a multistep method but rather an extension of object orientation into the time dimension: The central idea is that the task architecture should reflect concurrency that exists in the problem.

The tutorial follows the presenter's recent book *Design of multithreaded software: The entity-life modeling approach* [1] but uses Ada terminology. ELM was originally developed with Ada tasking in mind but works with Real-time Java as well. The tutorial is illustrated with multiple Ada examples.

2. TOPIC

Entity-life modeling (ELM) is an approach for designing multitask software for *reactive* systems, that is, systems that respond to events in the environment as they occur. This includes many real-time systems from automotive cruise controllers to automated factories as well as interactive systems from self-serve gas pumps to travel-reservation systems.

A *task architecture* consists of tasks and protected objects. ELM's central idea is that the architecture should reflect concurrency that exists in the problem. To this end, the architect identifies sequences of event occurrences in the problem domain that unfold independently or nearly so. Such sequences are called *event threads*. An event thread can often be related intuitively to an entity in the problem, such as an elevator cabin or a train. A human user can also be an entity and have a corresponding event thread. Each task is based on an event thread but event threads can also be implemented by means of interrupt or event handling.

ELM's goal is to eliminate pointless concurrency as when – for no good reason – a single input visits a number of tasks one after the other. ELM does not address the parallelization of algorithms but in no way precludes it; tasks executing in parallel on different processors are very much in ELM's spirit.

The tutorial generally follows the chapters in [1]. After an introduction of ELM and its purpose (Ch. 1), we cover relevant Ada tasking features (Ch. 2). We then recapitulate state diagramming with an emphasis on concepts relevant to ELM (Ch. 3). An introduction to ELM's conceptual apparatus (Ch. 4) follows, after which we discuss two ELM design patterns for basing tasks on the activities identified in a state model (Ch. 5).

Next we compare two *event-thread patterns* used to capture resource sharing in the problem domain (Ch. 6). They exhibit an interesting duality where the architect usually has two ways of looking at the problem leading to two different software solutions, potentially with quite different properties.

Finally, we discuss the important case where individual resource-user entities in the domain need exclusive access to two or more shared resources at once (Ch. 7). ELM puts such problems on a form that exposes the resource allocation and release so that appropriate deadlock prevention techniques can be applied and implemented in the task logic.

3. OUTLINE

1. Introduction

    Task architecture

    Reactive software

    Basing tasks on concurrency in the problem domain

    ELM concepts

2. Overview of tasking features in Ada

    Timing events

    Protected objects

      Protected entries; condition synchronization

      Requeue

      Protected objects for controlling access to domain resources

      Semaphore, Monitor, State-machine, and *Queue* POs

    Asynchronous transfer of control

3. State modeling as a basis for the design of reactive software

    Events and event threads

    Actions

    Activities

    Software activities as justification for tasks.

4. ELM concepts

    Essential events

      Events shared by domain and software

      Time events

      Essential events detected by the software alone:

        resource allocation, end of computation

    Event threads and entities

    Event-thread models

    Co-occurrence, optimality

    Event-thread / task types

5. Design patterns basing tasks on state models

    State machines without software activities

      Ex.: Window elevator, bicycle odometer

    State machines with software activities

      Sequential-activities pattern

        Ex.: Home heating

      Concurrent-activities pattern

        Ex.: Cruise control, weather buoy

    Communicating state machines

      Ex.: Toy-car factory, assembly-line workstations

6. Event-thread patterns for *resource sharing*

    Resource-*user*-thread pattern and resource-*guard*-thread pattern

    Duality between the patterns

      Ex.: Bank-office queuing, remote temperature sensor,

        home heater

    Repository problems

    Ex.: Elevator bank

7. Simultaneous exclusive access to multiple resources

    Deadlock problem

    Deadlock prevention

      - Partial ordering of resources

      - Limiting the number of competing resource users

      - Eliminating indefinite waiting

        Ex.: Dining philosophers

      Ex.: Switchyard

        Deadlock potential and prevention

      Ex.: Flexible manufacturing system

        Deadlock potential and prevention

        Software solutions

8. Summary.

4. PRESENTER'S BACKGROUND

Dr. Bo Sandén began his career as a software developer in industry and had opportunities to study and design multithreaded software. 1986-87 he was a Visiting Associate Professor in the pioneering software-engineering program at the Wang Institute, Tyngsboro, MA. As an Associate Professor at George Mason University, Fairfax, VA 1987-1996, he helped create a masters program in software systems engineering and taught design and led capstone projects with a focus on concurrent software. Since 1996 he is a Professor of Computer Science at Colorado Technical University in Colorado Springs, where he has taught at the undergraduate and master's levels and now exclusively teaches and directs student research in the Doctor of Computer Science program.

Dr. Sandén is the inventor of entity-life modeling and the author of "Design of multithreaded software: The entity-life modeling approach." He gave a number of tutorials on ELM in the mid-90s: ACM Professional Development Seminar 1994, Washington Ada Symposium 1994, 1995, 1996; TRI-Ada 1994, 1995, 1996. Since then he has taught ELM at Colorado Tech and externally, and published a number of articles on the topic primarily in the IEEE magazines. His tutorial on ELM at Ada Europe 2012 was well attended.

5. INTENDED AUDIENCE

Architects, designers, and programmers of real-time and interactive software as well as software-engineering academics and students interested in concurrency will understand and eventually learn the ELM way of designing reactive, multitask software.

If tasking is considered an "advanced" aspect of Ada, the level of the tutorial is ***advanced***. It assumes a general knowledge of tasking or threading.

6. REFERENCE

[1] Sandén, B. I. 2011. *Design of Multithreaded Software: The Entity-Life Modeling Approach.* IEEE Computer Society Press/Wiley.

Leading-Edge Ada Verification Technologies:
Highly Automated Ada Contract Checking using Bakar Kiasan

Jason Belt   Patrice Chalin   Robby   John Hatcliff

SAnToS Laboratory
Computing and Information Sciences
Kansas State University, USA

{belt,chalin,robby,hatcliff}@ksu.edu

ABSTRACT
This tutorial presents a new approach to Spark/Ada contract checking using Bakar Kiasan—a highly automated, evidence-based symbolic execution tool. Bakar Kiasan aims to lower the barrier of entry and reduce the burden of engineers as they specify and verify Ada contracts. Even in the absence of contracts, Bakar Kiasan can check code for possible runtime exceptions and provide visualizations of semantic constraints along paths through procedures. As engineers progressively add contracts, Bakar Kiasan can verify the consistency of code and contracts, thus providing increased confidence, often proportional to the efforts made to capture fuller behavioral specifications via contracts. Bakar Kiasan also provides compositional checking; that is, it can be used on incomplete systems, where contracts are only present for some program components (which may not even have been implemented). This allows contract checking to be used as the program is being developed starting early in the software development process.

Bakar Kiasan provides helpful feedback and evidence of its verification results. For example, it automatically generates counter examples as program test cases for illustrating how contracts are violated (this is very helpful when debugging code/contracts), as well as providing various visualization cues, for example, highlighting problematic code or contract segments similar to how modern Integrated Development Environments (IDEs) illustrate compile (type) errors. Kiasan also generates test cases for illustrating how contracts are satisfied, which is helpful for understanding code/contracts or confirming how a program should behave. Bakar Kiasan is integrated in the Eclipse IDE as a plug-in, and an integration with the GNAT Programming Studio (GPS) is currently being developed in collaboration with AdaCore.

This tutorial includes a gentle introduction to symbolic execution and case studies on how Bakar Kiasan has been applied to, for example, industrial code and contracts supplied by our collaborators at Rockwell Collins. During the tutorial, attendees equipped with a laptop will be able to install and apply Bakar Kiasan to some sample code/contracts to get a hands-on experience of Spark/Ada checking using Bakar Kiasan. The tutorial will also provide an introduction to a companion tool, Bakar Alir, that provides rich visualizations of information flow through Spark programs, which can be useful to developers when writing Spark "derives" clauses and reasoning about end-to-end security and separation policies.

Acknowledgements
The development of Bakar Kiasan is partially funded by the US National Science Foundation (NSF) CAREER grant #0644288, the US Air Force Office of Scientific Research (AFOSR), the Natural Sciences and Engineering Research Council (NSERC) of Canada grant #261573, and Rockwell Collins. Any opinions, findings, and conclusions or recommendations expressed in this tutorial are those of the presenters and do not necessarily reflect the views of the previously mentioned institutions.

Categories and Subject Descriptors
D.2.1 [**Software Engineering**]: Requirements/Specifications -- *languages, methodologies, tools.* D.2.4 [**Software Engineering**]: Software/Program Verification -- *assertion checkers, class invariants, correctness proofs, formal methods, programming by contract.* D.2.5 [**Software Engineering**]: Testing and Debugging – symbolic execution. F.3.1 [**Logics and Meaning of Programs**]: Specifying and Verifying and Reasoning about Programs – *assertions, invariants, logics of programs, mechanical verification, pre- and post-conditions, specification techniques.* F.4.1 [**Mathematical Logic and Formal Languages**] Mathematical Logic -- *mechanical theorem proving.*

General Terms
Languages, Theory, Verification.

Keywords
SPARK, Ada, symbolic execution, software contracts

Speaker Biographies
Jason Belt is a Ph.D. Candidate at the Computing and Information Sciences (CIS) Department at Kansas State University (KSU). He received his M.S. from KSU CIS and his research focuses on software verification and analysis. For his Ph.D. work, he develops Bakar Kiasan -- a symbolic execution, evidence-based program verification tool targeting Spark Ada.

Dr. Patrice Chalin is an Associate Professor at KSU CIS who has been doing research in specification and programming language semantics as well as program verification since the early 90s. He has also been active in the development of verification tooling including JmlEclipse, an IDE for Java supporting the Java Modeling Language. More recent efforts in language design, semantics, tooling and tutorials have come to focus on Spark/Ada and its symbolic execution.

Dr. John Hatcliff is a University Distinguished Professor at KSU CIS. Hatcliff's research focuses on developing software design and verification tools for embedded security systems and integrated medical systems. He has been Principal Investigator on a number of Department of Defense research grants focusing on safety-critical software. He is a co-recipient of a 2010 International Conference on Software Engineering (ICSE) Most Influential Paper (MIP) award and 2010 ACM Special Interest Group on Software Engineering (SIGSOFT) Impact award; these awards are typically given to a research paper that is deemed to make the most significant contribution to software engineering theory and practice a decade after the paper is originally published.

Dr. Robby is an Associate Professor at KSU CIS. His main research interests are in the area of software specification and verification techniques. He received a NSF CAREER award in 2007 for his work on formal software analysis for open systems, which has resulted in the development of the highly automated Kiasan symbolic execution-based program verification framework that is applicable to various application domains and software artifact level of abstractions such as software model, specification, and code. He is also a co-recipient of the 2010 ICSE MIP and the 2010 ACM SIGSOFT Impact awards.This tutorial includes a gentle introduction to symbolic execution and case studies on how Bakar Kiasan has been applied to, for example, industrial code and contracts supplied by our collaborators at Rockwell Collins

Leading-edge Ada Verification Technologies: Combining Testing and Verification with GNATTest and GNATProve – the Hi-Lite Project

Johannes Kanig
AdaCore
46 rue d'Amsterdam
F-75009 Paris (France)
kanig@adacore.com

ABSTRACT

We give a hands-on introduction to the tools GNATtest and GNATprove, both developed at AdaCore in the Hi-Lite research project. They allow to do verification of Ada 2012 contracts through testing and formal verification, and also allow a combination of the results of both tools.

The tutorial will contain a very short introduction to Ada 2012, and attendees will write a small example on which they can play with GNATtest to develop test cases, and GNATprove to do some formal verification.

Categories and Subject Descriptors

F.3.1 [**Logics and Meaning of Programs**]: Specifying and Verifying and Reasoning about Programs—*Pre- and Postconditions, Mechanical Verification*; D.2.4 [**Software Engineering**]: Software/Program Verification—*Formal Methods, Programming by Contract*; D.3.4 [**Programming Languages**]: Processors—*Compilers*

Keywords

Compiler technology, formal verification, testing

1. CONTENTS OF THE TUTORIAL

This tutorial focusses on the two verification tools GNATtest and GNATprove, both developed at AdaCore as part of the the Hi-Lite [2] research project.

GNATtest is a tool which generates a unit test harness for any Ada-program. For each subprogram, test stubs are generated which can then be implemented by the developer. GNATtest generates a test harness, which executes all the tests and gives a summary of failed or passed tests. In case of a failed test, Ada 2012 contracts help to determine if the problem is in the test or the code to be tested.

In addition, GNATtest supports the GNAT-specific aspect `Test_Case`, which allows to split the tests of a subprogram into different cases. GNATtest will check whether each test actually tests the subprogram in the specified situation.

GNATprove, on the other hand, can provide formal proof that a subprogram does not contain runtime errors, and that implements its Ada 2012 contract. While GNATtest supports the full Ada 2012 language, GNATprove can only analyze a restricted, but still quite large, subset of Ada, which notably excludes pointers and exceptions.

One of the novelties of the Hi-Lite approach is that the results of GNATprove and GNATtest can be combined in a sound way, so that the most suitable verification method can be chosen for any given subprogram. In particular, and in contrast with most existing proof tools, one does not need to apply proof on the entire program to obtain meaningful results. The combination will not be shown in the tutorial.

2. STATUS OF THE PRESENTED TOOLS

GNATtest is officially part of the GNAT GPL and GNAT Pro distributions. GNATprove is still a prototype, and is distributed separately [1].

3. PREREQUISITE KNOWLEDGE OR SKILLS

The audience should have a basic understanding of Ada to benefit most from the tutorial. Familiarity with the Pre- and Postcondition aspects of Ada 2012 will also make it easier to understand the tutorial, but we will explain these.

4. INTENDED AUDIENCE

The tutorial will be most interesting for engineers and students who want to see new technologies that may be part of their workflow in the future.

5. THE PRESENTER

Johannes Kanig holds engineering degrees of the Ecole Centrale Paris, France and the Technical University of Dresden, Germany. He has done his PhD in formal methods at the french research institute INRIA near Paris. Johannes is Software engineer and works on the static analysis tools developed at AdaCore, namely CodePeer and GNATprove.

6. REFERENCES

[1] GNATprove GPL release.
   http://www.open-do.org/projects/hi-lite/gnatprove.
[2] Hi-Lite: Simplifying the use of formal methods.
   http://www.open-do.org/projects/hi-lite/.

HILT'12, December 2–6, 2012, Boston, Massachusetts, USA.
ACM 978-1-4503-1505-0/12/12.

Safety of Embedded Software

Professor Nancy Leveson
Massachusetts
Institute of Technology
33-334
77 Massachusetts Avenue
Cambridge, MA 02139
1-617-258-0505
leveson@mit.edu

Cody Harrison Fleming
Massachusetts
Institute of Technology
33-407
77 Massachusetts Avenue
Cambridge, MA 02139
1-617-253-4519
chf44@mit.edu

John Thomas
Massachusetts
Institute of Technology
33-407
77 Massachusetts Avenue
Cambridge, MA 02139
1-617-253-4519
jthomas4@mit.edu

ABSTRACT

Traditional safety techniques were created 40-50 years ago for electro-mechanical systems. The underlying assumptions of these techniques about the cause of accidents (e.g., component failure) do not match software nor do they match the types of accidents we are having that are related to software. As a result, a large number of accidents are now related to software, although usually the pilot (for aircraft) or other human operators are blamed. Often, the software design leads to the operator errors. We will describe the problems with software that are leading to accidents (primarily in the requirements) and how to deal with them. Most of the current approaches rely on reducing "failures" although software does not fail. Something else is needed.

In the tutorial we will present a new accident causality model (STAMP) and teach how to use a new hazard analysis technique (STPA) based on it that can be used on complex, software-intensive systems. The topics will include how to generate software safety requirements from an STPA hazard analysis and how to design software that does not induce human error. The tutorial will be based on a new book, *Engineering a Safer World* by Nancy Leveson and published in January 2012 by MIT Press.

Categories and Subject Descriptors

D.2.1 [Software Engineering]: Requirements/Specifications—Methodologies, Tools

General Terms

Algorithms, Management, Measurement, Documentation, Design, Human Factors, Theory, Verification

Keywords

System safety, systems theory, control theory, hazard analysis, complex systems, component interaction, requirements, specification

HILT'12, December 2–6, 2012, Boston, Massachusetts, USA.
ACM 978-1-4503-1505-0/12/12.

Developing Verified Programs with Dafny

K. Rustan M. Leino
Microsoft Research
Redmond, WA, USA
leino@microsoft.com

ABSTRACT

Reasoning about programs is a fundamental skill that every software engineer needs. This tutorial provides participants an opportunity to get hands-on experience with Dafny [6], a tool that can help develop this skill.

Dafny is a programming language and state-of-the-art program verifier. The language is type-safe and sequential, and it includes common imperative features, dynamic object allocation, and inductive datatypes. It also includes specification constructs like pre- and postconditions, which let a programmer record the intended behavior of the program along with the executable code that is supposed to cause that behavior. Because the Dafny verifier runs continuously in the background, the consistency of a program and its specifications is always enforced.

In this tutorial, I give a taste of how to use Dafny in program development. This includes an overview of Dafny, basics of writing specifications, how to debug verification attempts, and how to formulate and prove lemmas.

Dafny has been used to verify a number of challenging algorithms, including Schorr-Waite graph marking [6], Floyd's "tortoise and hare" cycle-detection algorithm, and snapshotable trees with iterators. Dafny is also being used in teaching, with over 100,000 program-verification attempts submitted to the online version of the tool. Dafny was a popular choice in the VSTTE 2012 program verification competition, where two of the Dafny teams were among the competition's 6 medalists. Its open-source implementation has also been used as a foundation for other verification tools.

More information is found from the Dafny project page, http://research.microsoft.com/dafny and in the references below. Binary downloads and sources are available from http://dafny.codeplex.com. The tool can also be run on the web at http://rise4fun.com/dafny, where there is an online version of the tutorial [3].

Categories and Subject Descriptors

D.2.2 [**SOFTWARE ENGINEERING**]: Design Tools and Techniques

General Terms

Verification

Keywords

Reasoning about programs, formal correctness, specifications, verification, programming tools, auto-active verification, Dafny

1. REFERENCES

[1] L. Herbert, K. R. M. Leino, and J. Quaresma. Using Dafny, an automatic program verifier. In B. Meyer and M. Nordio, editors, *LASER 2012*, volume 7682 of *LNCS*, pages 156–181. Springer, 2012.

[2] B. Jacobs, J. Smans, and F. Piessens. VeriFast: Imperative programs as proofs. In *VS-Tools workshop at VSTTE 2010*, Aug. 2010.

[3] J. Koenig and K. R. M. Leino. Getting started with Dafny: A guide. In T. Nipkow, O. Grumberg, and B. Hauptmann, editors, *Software Safety and Security: Tools for Analysis and Verification*, volume 33 of *NATO Science for Peace and Security Series D: Information and Communication Security*, pages 152–181. IOS Press, 2012. Summer School Marktoberdorf 2011 lecture notes.

[4] C. Le Goues, K. R. M. Leino, and M. Moskal. The Boogie Verification Debugger (tool paper). In G. Barthe, A. Pardo, and G. Schneider, editors, *Software Engineering and Formal Methods - 9th International Conference, SEFM 2011*, volume 7041 of *LNCS*, pages 407–414. Springer, Nov. 2011.

[5] K. R. M. Leino. Specification and verification of object-oriented software. In M. Broy, W. Sitou, and T. Hoare, editors, *Engineering Methods and Tools for Software Safety and Security*, volume 22 of *NATO Science for Peace and Security Series D: Information and Communication Security*, pages 231–266. IOS Press, 2009. Summer School Marktoberdorf 2008 lecture notes.

[6] K. R. M. Leino. Dafny: An automatic program verifier for functional correctness. In E. M. Clarke and A. Voronkov, editors, *LPAR-16*, volume 6355 of *LNCS*, pages 348–370. Springer, Apr. 2010.

[7] K. R. M. Leino. Automating induction with an SMT solver. In V. Kuncak and A. Rybalchenko, editors, *Verification, Model Checking, and Abstract Interpretation - 13th International Conference, VMCAI 2012*, volume 7148 of *LNCS*, pages 315–331. Springer, Jan. 2012.

[8] K. R. M. Leino and M. Moskal. Usable auto-active verification. In T. Ball, L. Zuck, and N. Shankar,

editors, *UV10 (Usable Verification) workshop.* `http://fm.csl.sri.com/UV10/`, Nov. 2010.

[9] B. Meyer. *Object-oriented Software Construction.* Series in Computer Science. Prentice-Hall International, 1988.

Service-Oriented Architecture (SOA) Concepts and Implementations

Ricky E. Sward
The MITRE Corporation
1155 Academy Park Loop
Colorado Springs, CO 80910
rsward@mitre.org

Jeff Boleng
The Software Engineering Institute
Carnegie Mellon University
4500 Fifth Avenue
Pittsburgh, PA 15213
jlboleng@sei.cmu.edu

ABSTRACT

This tutorial explains how to implement a Service-Oriented Architecture (SOA) for reliable systems using an Enterprise Service Bus (ESB) and the Ada Web Server (AWS). The first part of the tutorial describes terms of Service-Oriented Architectures (SOA) including service, service registry, service provider, service consumer, Service Oriented Architecture Protocol (SOAP), and Web Service Description Language (WSDL). This tutorial also presents principles of SOA including loose coupling, encapsulation, composability of web services, and statelessness of web services. The tutorial also covers the benefits of SOA and organizations that are supporting SOA infrastructure. The second part of the tutorial covers the Enterprise Service Bus (ESB) including definitions, capabilities, benefits and drawbacks. The tutorial discusses the difference between SOA and an ESB, as well as some of the commercially available ESB solutions on the market. The Mule ESB is explored in more detail and several examples are given. In the third part, the tutorial covers the Ada Web Server (AWS) built using the Ada programming language. The tutorial covers the capabilities of AWS and explains how to build and install AWS. The tutorial explains how to build an AWS server and include the server in an Ada application. The tutorial demonstrates how to build a call back function in AWS and build a response to a SOAP message. Finally, the tutorial explains how to connect an AWS server to an ESB endpoint. AWS is a key component to building a SOA for a reliable system. This capability allows the developer to expose services in a high-integrity system using the Ada and SPARK programming languages.

Categories and Subject Descriptors

D.2.11 [Software Engineering]: Software Architectures

Keywords

Service Oriented Architectures; Ada

1. DETAILED OUTLINE

1. Introduction and Background
2. Part 1 – Service-Oriented Architecture
   a. SOA Background Terminology: XML, XML Document, XSD, XSLT
   b. SOA Terminology: Service, Registry, Provider, Consumer, WSDL, SOAP, SLA
   c. SOA Message Patterns: Request/Response, Publish/Subscribe
   d. SOA Orchestration and Web Service Security
   e. Principles of SOA
   f. Benefits of SOA
   g. SOA Organizations: W3C, OASIS
3. Part 2 – Enterprise Service Bus (ESB)
   a. ESB description and terminology
   b. Commercial ESB options
   c. ESB's and SOA
   d. Mule ESB Case Study and examples
      i. Mule endpoints
      ii. Mule configuration file
4. Part 3 – Ada Web Server (AWS)
   a. AWS definitions and capabilities
   b. Building and Installing AWS
   c. Building an AWS web server
   d. Building a call-back function
   e. AWS server example
   f. AWS and WSDLs
5. Connecting AWS to Mule
   a. Configuration file
   b. Building an Ada web service
   c. Exposing an Ada web service
   d. Example
6. Conclusions

2. ABOUT THE PRESENTERS

Ricky E. "Ranger" Sward is a Lead Information Systems Engineer for the MITRE Corporation in Colorado Springs, CO, USA. He currently supports the Air Force A2U Unmanned Systems ISR Innovations Branch working to integrate full-motion video initiatives for unmanned aircraft systems. He is also supporting an internal MITRE research project on composable widgets using a Service Oriented Architecture (SOA) implementation. Ranger retired from the Air Force in August 2006 after a 21 year career as a Communications and Computer officer. He taught at the US Air Force Academy for 10 years where he taught courses such as Software Engineering and Unmanned Aircraft Systems. He has a B.S. and an M.S. in Computer Science, as well as a Ph.D. in Computer Engineering. He is currently Chair of ACM SIGAda.

Jeff Boleng is a research scientist in the Advanced Mobile Systems group at the Software Engineering Institute, Carnegie Mellon University, in Pittsburgh, PA, USA. His current research focus is enabling rich computing applications and data at the tactical edge. He is also researching techniques for widespread software portability and attack surface characterization of mobile devices. His past operational Air Force Experience includes evaluating and implementing SOA solutions for command and control and knowledge management applications. He is a 1991 graduate of the US Air Force Academy and has an M.S. and Ph.D. in Mathematical and Computer Sciences from Colorado School of Mines.

HILT'12, December 2–6, 2012, Boston, Massachusetts, USA.
ACM 978-1-4503-1505-0/12/12.

Tutorial: Multicore Programming using Divide-and-Conquer and Work Stealing

S. Tucker Taft
AdaCore
24 Muzzey Street 3rd Fl
Lexington, MA 02421
+1-781-750-8068 x220
taft@adacore.com

ABSTRACT

This tutorial is aimed at engineers and students who are interested in learning more about parallel programming, particularly for systems with growing numbers of physical processors or cores.

Categories and Subject Descriptors

D.1.3 [**Programming Techniques**]: Concurrent Programming – *parallel programming.*

General Terms

Algorithms, Performance, Languages,.

Keywords

Multicore Programming, Divide and Conquer, Work Stealing.

1. AUDIENCE FOR TUTORIAL

This tutorial is aimed at engineers and students who are interested in learning more about parallel programming, particularly for systems with growing numbers of physical processors or cores.

2. PREREQUISITE SKILLS

Some familiarity with threads, mutual exclusion, synchronization, scheduling, etc. will be useful.

3. TUTORIAL TOPICS

This tutorial will introduce the attendee to some of the issues of parallel programming for multicore systems. We will discuss some of the models used for creating and then managing efficiently large numbers of *picothreads*. The tutorial will first cover the basic technique of *divide and conquer* as it applies to splitting up computations into large numbers of separate sub-computations. We will provide examples using Intel's Cilk+ [1] language as well as using ParaSail [2], a new parallel programming language. The tutorial will then go on to investigate the *work-stealing* scheduling mechanism used by the Cilk+ runtime, Intel's Threaded Basic Blocks library [3], as well as the ParaSail virtual machine. Work-stealing [4] is an efficient way to handle the large number of very small *picothreads* created in abundance by these parallel programming technologies. We will end with a short discussion of heterogeneous parallel programming, using auxiliary chips such as Graphics Processing Units (GPUs) as general purpose processors (GPGPU) [5].

4. REFERENCES

[1] Intel Corporation, *Intel® Cilk++ SDK Programmer's Guide*, 2009, http://software.intel.com/file/23634 (retrieved 10-Oct-2012).

[2] Taft, S. T., *Designing ParaSail, a new programming language*, blog, 2009 http://parasail-programming-language.blogspot.com (retrieved 10-Oct-2012)

[3] Intel Corporation, *Intel Threaded Building Blocks for Open Source,* http://threadingbuildingblocks.org/ (retrieved 10-Oct-2012).

[4] Blumofe, R. D., Leisersen, C. E., "Scheduling Multithreaded Computations by Work Stealing," *Journal of the ACM*, pp. 720–748, September, 1999, http://supertech.csail.mit.edu/papers/steal.pdf (retrieved 10-Oct-2012)

[5] Harris, M., "About GPGPU.org," *General Purpose Computation on Graphics Hardware*, 2012, http://gpgpu.org/about (retrieved 10-Oct-2012).

Tutorial Overview: Understanding Dynamic Memory Management in Safety Critical Java

Kelvin Nilsen, Chief Technology Officer Java
Atego Systems
5930 Cornerstone Court West, Suite 250
San Diego, CA 92121
(+1) 801-756-4821
kelvin.nilsen@atego.com

ABSTRACT

In spite of the high-level abstraction benefits of automatic tracing garbage collection, current prevailing sentiment within the safety certification community is that a simpler memory model is required for the most rigorous levels of software safety certification. Thus, the draft JSR-302 specification for safety critical Java relies on scope-based memory allocation rather than tracing garbage collection. The scoped memory model for JSR-302 is a simplification of the RTSJ model. JSR-302 enforces a strict hierarchy of scopes and distinguishes private scopes, which can be seen only by one thread, from mission scopes, which can be accessed by all the threads that comprise a mission, including threads running within inner-nested sub-missions. The hierarchical memory structure allows implementations to guarantee the absence of memory fragmentation for scope management, unlike the Real-Time Specification for Java from which the JSR-302 specification was derived.

In the absence of block structure, it is more difficult in Java to safely manage references to stack-allocated objects than in Ada. While the simplified hierarchical management of scoped memory that is part of JSR-302 addresses memory fragmentation concerns, it does not guarantee the absence of dangling pointers. As with the Real-Time Specification for Java, JSR-302 requires a run-time check to enforce that no reference assignment creates a relationship whereby an outer-nested object is allowed to point to an inner-nested object. This rule assures the absence of dangling pointers, but it introduces a different problem: every assignment to a reference field must be accompanied by a run-time check to validate the appropriate scope nesting relationship. This run-time check will throw a run-time exception if the assignment is deemed inappropriate.

The safety certification evidence for a given safety-critical Java program must therefore include an argument for every reference assignment that it will not cause the program to abort with a run-time exception. Furthermore, the certification evidence must prove that sufficient memory is available to reliably execute each safety-critical task in the system.

This tutorial provides an overview of dynamic memory management in Safety Critical Java and describes two annotation systems that have been designed to support static (compile-time) enforcement of memory safety properties. The first annotation system is described in an appendix to the draft JSR-302 standard. This relatively simple annotation system, which is not considered normative, serves to demonstrate that memory safety can be statically proven without requiring extensive annotations throughout existing library code. The second annotation system is the system implemented in Perc Pico. This annotation system, which is much richer than the draft JSR-302 annotation, has been in experimental use for over five years. During that time, tens of thousands of lines of experimental application code have been developed, with the experience motivating a variety of refinements to the original design.

Categories and Subject Descriptors

D.3.2 [**Language Classifications**] Concurrent, distributed, and parallel languages, Object-oriented languages, Java; D.2.4 [**Software/Program Verification**]: Correctness proofs, Reliability, Validation; D.2.7 [**Distribution, Maintenance, and Enhancement**]: Corrections, Enhancement, Extensibility, Portability; D.2.11 [**Software Architectures**]: Data abstraction, Information hiding, Languages, Patterns; D.2.13 [**Reusable Software**]: Reusable libraries, Reusable models

General Terms

Design, Reliability, Standardization, Verification

Keywords

Java, Dynamic Storage Management, Real-Time, Safety-Critical, Mission-Critical, High-Integrity Systems, Object Oriented Development, Mixed-Model Deployment

1. INTRODUCTION

The use of Java [1] in real-time systems has taken various forms over the years. The earliest commercial approaches to real-time Java (circa 1997) used standard edition Java APIs with real-time garbage collection [2]. This preserves the high-level abstractions of Java that make it inherently safer than, for example, C and C++. Later, in 2000, the Real-Time Specification for Java (RTSJ) introduced new mechanisms to support higher degrees of determinism in real-time Java [3]. Unfortunately, the RTSJ represented a step backwards in terms of software safety, abstraction, and maintainability. While the RTSJ mechanisms make it possible to write Java programs that equal the real-time latency guarantees of assembly language and C, RTSJ programmers must exercise an abundance of caution in order to avoid illegal memory access errors, memory fragmentation errors, out-of-memory conditions, and priority inversion problems. Faced with these difficult development challenges, the benefits of RTSJ over more traditional legacy languages like C and Ada have been unclear [4, 5]. As a result, even ten years after publication of the official RTSJ "standard", this technology has not been deployed in any large-scale Java applications.

This motivated several efforts to simplify the RTSJ programming model [6-9]. Work on a standard safety-critical Java specification for Java has been ongoing since the Open Group hosted an initial meeting on this topic in July 2003. Early discussions within the Open Group resulted in an architectural framework and a set of annotations to enable modular composition and certification of independently developed safety-critical Java components [10]. These approaches were first implemented in the commercial PERC Pico product by Aonix (which merged in 2010 with Artisan to become Atego) in 2007 [11].

In 2006, the Open Group's safety-critical Java effort transformed itself into the JSR-302 expert group of the Java Community Process. With this transition, new parties joined the process, and these parties brought a shift away from some of the Open Group's earlier directions. In particular, there was a desire to maintain greater compatibility with the RTSJ. The resulting JSR-302 specification, which is now nearly complete, represents a compromise between many alternative perspectives and objectives [12].

This tutorial discusses two distinct semantic models for safety-critical code written in the Java language. Since Java is an object-oriented programming language, it is very difficult to write code in normal Java style without allocating temporary objects. While it might be possible to preallocate reusable object pools during mission initialization, this burdens software developers with managing problems of memory fragmentation, dangling pointers, and memory conflicts between multiple users who both might believe they have exclusive access to the object. Further, reusable object pools don't work well for immutable data types such as java.lang.String, objects with variable internal size such as java.math.BigInteger, nor data types that depend on a parameterized constructor to establish the initial state of the instantiation. The goal of both semantic models is to deliver as many of the traditional benefits of Java and to support the traditional styles of normal Java development as much as possible.

The two semantic models correspond to a very restrictive run-time environment that manages temporary memory using scope-based allocation instead of tracing garbage collection. We refer to these as the *Annotated JSR-302* and *PERC Pico* semantic models. Both use Java annotations to augment the standard Java type system. Annotations (also known as *Metadata*) were added to Java with the J2SE 5.0 release in September, 2004 [13]. Annotations are recognized in Java source code by names beginning with an @ character. Third party tools, such as might be provided by a vendor of a safety-critical Java development tool chain, are able to associate special meanings with the use of particular annotations.

Annotated JSR-302 provides improved abstraction over traditional JSR-302 in that a static checker enforces that the application code will not throw an IllegalAssignmentError. The checker relies on the presence of optional annotations in the source code. Even with

Annotated JSR-302, programmers are required to explicitly manage the creation, sizing, entry into, and exit from scopes.

As with Annotated JSR-302, the *PERC Pico* semantic model relies on the presence of annotations to clarify the programmer's intentions with regards to scoped memory relationships. Unlike JSR-302, the use of annotations in this semantic model is not optional. Annotation enforcement with PERC Pico is more than simply checking that the programmer is doing the right thing. With PERC Pico, annotation checking interacts with native code generation to make the annotations valid. For example, if the annotations on a body of code indicate that a particular temporary object may be referenced from external scopes, the compiler automatically arranges that the memory allocated for that object is taken from a scope that lives as long as those external scopes.

2. JSR-302 OVERVIEW

A JSR-302 application is structured as one or more missions, running either in sequence or concurrently. Each mission has a mission memory to hold all of the temporary objects that are to be shared between the independently executing threads that comprise the mission. JSR-302 threads are embodied as periodic event handlers, asynchronous event handlers, or ongoing threads. Each thread has a stack of private memory areas to hold the temporary objects required for its computations.

One of the design ideals of the JSR-302 specification was to maintain compatibility with RTSJ. This is most notable in its approach to allocation of memory for short-lived objects. Like the RTSJ, the JSR-302 specification requires that programmers explicitly manage memory scopes. Each memory scope has a size that must be determined by the application programmer. A JSR-302 program enters a scope by executing one of several possible standard APIs. Once entered, subsequent new object allocations are, by default, satisfied by taking the memory from the currently entered scope. After all threads exit the scope, all of the objects allocated within the scope are discarded and their memory is reclaimed.

Unlike the RTSJ, JSR-302 supports only two very restrictive scope types. Both scope types are instantiated only by infrastructure, only in particular contexts at particular times. A MissionMemory scope is instantiated and sized only during the initialization of a new mission. A PrivateMemory scope is only instantiated when an event handler begins to run, or when user code requests to enter a new private memory area. These restrictions on the generality of RTSJ scopes simplify the run-time execution model and make it possible for implementations of the JSR-302 specification to guarantee that memory fragmentation does not prevent the timely and reliable creation of new memory areas, unlike the RTSJ.

As with the RTSJ, JSR-302 programmers are responsible for honoring the restriction that objects residing within a particular memory scope are never allowed to refer to objects residing within more inner-nested memory scopes. At each point in a program's execution that this rule would be violated, an IllegalAssignmentError exception is thrown instead.

Clearly, it is undesirable that a safety-critical program might terminate with a run-time error due to an inappropriate pointer assignment. In its current form, the JSR-302 specification states that it is ultimately the developers' responsibility to assure the absence of illegal assignments in their safety-critical Java programs. Vendors of safety-critical Java programming tools and run-time environments are encouraged to provide tools to help programmers prove the absence of these exceptions. And the draft specification describes an optional annotation system and enforcement tool that can be applied to safety-critical applications at the discretion of developers or project leads to guarantee the absence of these exceptions. This annotation system is simpler and less expressive than the system that had been designed during the earlier Open Group standardization efforts.

Figure 1 provides an example program written according to the rules of JSR-302, using the optional annotations to enforce scope assignment safety. This program fragment represents code that might be executed within a mission's constructor to initialize a cryptography key.

The excerpted code omits certain details. For example, it does not show the annotation that requires instances of TheMission class to reside within the "TM" scope. The constructor for TheMission is shown at the bottom of the figure.

The sample code illustrates the complexity of managing explicit scopes as is required to perform certain intermediate computations in temporary memory that can be reclaimed upon termination of the constructor. This sample code creates and enters a private memory area to hold an AbsoluteTime object, a Random object, three BigInteger objects, and an AssignCryptoKey object[1]. Note that the calculation of the private memory's scope size must account for internal objects which are allocated within the constructors of AbsoluteTime, Random, or BigInteger instances. This information may not be known without scrutiny of the respective constructor implementations. Reliance on this information violates best practice guidelines for information hiding and encapsulation.

In this sample code, the temporary CalculateCryptoKey and SizeEstimator objects that are allocated by the TheMission constructor are placed in MissionMemory and live there until the mission itself terminates. It would have been preferable to place these objects also in temporary memory, but it is very difficult to do so using the JSR-302 programming conventions which were inherited from the RTSJ.

For comparison, a C implementation of a comparable memory model is represented by the code shown in Figure 2. This sample code assumes that libraries exist to perform similar actions in C that are performed by the existing Java libraries. The point of pre-

---

[1]. It is not common for RTSJ developers to compute scope sizes with this level of precision. Rather, RTSJ programmers tend to guess at required scope sizes and then test whether they guessed large enough. One reviewer of this paper, in fact, suggested that the paper should replace the SizeEstimator calculations with the constant 4096, suggesting that "should be enough". Such practices are dangerous and brittle. The use of magic number constants to size scopes introduces a future software maintenance burden and a risk that some future deployment of this code on a new JVM platform, or with slightly different library implementations will result in an OutOfMemoryError. It is desirable to eliminate the need to review and validate that all such magic number constants are correct following every small change to the software.

```java
@SCJRestricted(INITIALIZATION)
public TheMission() {
  CalculateCryptoKey calculator =
     new CalculateCryptoKey(this);
  SizeEstimator z = new SizeEstimator();
  z.reserve(AbsoluteTime.class, 1);
  z.reserve(Random.class, 1);
  z.reserve(BigInteger.class, 3);
  z.reserveArray(20, byte.class);
  z.reserveArray(20, byte.class);
  z.reserveArray(40, byte.class);
  z.reserve(CalculateCryptoKey.AssignCryptoKey.class, 1);
  ((ManagedMemory) MemoryArea.getMemoryArea(this)).
  enterPrivateMemory(z.getEstimate(), calculator);
}


@Scope("TM") @SCJAllowed(members=true)
static class CalculateCryptoKey implements Runnable {

  TrainMission tm;
  public CalculateCryptoKey(TheMission the_mission) {
   tm = the_mission;
  }
  @DefineScope(name="TM.o", parent="TM")
  @Scope("TM.o") @SCJAllowed(members=true)
  static class AssignCryptoKey implements Runnable {
   TheMission tm;     // resides in scope "TM"
   BigInteger bi;     // resides in scope "TM.o"
   AssignCryptoKey(TrainMission tm, BigInteger bi) {
    this.tm = tm;
    this.bi = bi;
   }
   @RunsIn("TM")
   public void run() {
    // copy bi into the "TM" scope (from the "TM.o" scope)
    tm.crypto_key = bi.multiply(BigInteger.ONE);
   }
  }

  @RunsIn("TM.o")
  public void run() {
   AbsoluteTime now =
      javax.realtime.Clock.getRealtimeClock().getTime();
   Random r = new Random(now.getMilliseconds());
   BigInteger t1, t2, t3;
   t1 = new BigInteger(128, 24, r);
   t2 = new BigInteger(128, 24, r);
   t3 = t1.multiply(t2);
   AssignCryptoKey assigner =
      new AssignCryptoKey(tm, t3);
   MemoryArea.getMemoryArea(tm).
     executeInArea(assigner);
  }
}
```

Figure 1. JSR-302 Constructor for TheMission

senting this C version of the code is to clarify how a typical C programmer would arrange code so that the relevant objects are allocated in the appropriate stack memory locations. Note that the C version of BigInteger makes a reference to a separately allocated array of 8-bit characters to represent its integer encoding. The initializeMission() function links each BigInteger structure to the corresponding array. With C, there is no enforcement of scope safety. Programmers are responsible for assuring that referenced objects live at least as long as the pointers that refer to them. Also, note that this C code does not implement strong separation of concerns. The initializeMission() function directly manipulates the

```
typedef struct { char *digits;
 unsigned char avail_digits;
 unsigned char used_digits;
 unsigned char sign; } BigInteger;

typedef struct { BigInteger crypto_key; } TheMission;

TheMission tm;
char digits[40];

void initializeMission() {
 BigInteger t1, t2;
 char digits1[20], digits2[20];
 struct timespec now;
 longlong seed;
 clock_gettime(CLOCK_REALTIME, &now);
 seed = now.tv_nsec +
   (longlong) now.tv_sec * 1000000000;
 tm.crypto_key.digits = digits;  tm.avail_digits = 40;
 t1.digits = digits1; t1.avail_digits = 20;
 t2.digits = digits2; t2.avail_digits = 20;
 fillRandomBigInteger(&t1, 128, 24, &seed);
 fillRandomBigInteger(&t2, 128, 24, &seed);
 multiplyBigInteger(&t1, &t2, &(TheMission.crypto_key));
}
```

Figure 2. C initializer for TheMission

internals of the BigInteger data type.

3. PERC PICO OVERVIEW

The PERC Pico technology is based on the original system of annotations that had been developed in the Open Group's original safety-critical Java meetings. This annotation system provides increased expressive power and enables automatic determination of scope sizes. A sample constructor implementation written in the style of PERC Pico is shown in Figure 3.

Note that the code is much more concise and more readable than code written in the style of JSR-302. The PERC Pico compiler uses a sophisticated byte-code analyzer to trace the flow of each allocated object. Based on how the variable is used, it automatically determines the memory scope from which the allocation should be satisfied. For example, allocations assigned to a *captive-scoped* variable are always taken from an implicit local scope associated with execution of the current method. Within a constructor, variables assigned to *scoped* variables that are not *captive* are always taken from a special region of memory known as the *constructed scope*. The constructed scope is simply an expansion of the scope that holds the object being constructed. The reason the

```
@StaticAnalyzable
public TheMission() {
 @CaptiveScoped AbsoluteTime now;
 @CaptiveScoped r = new Random();
 @CaptiveScoped BigInteger t1, t2;
 now = javax.realtime.Clock.getRealtimeClock().getTime();
 Random r = new Random(now.getMilliseconds());
 assert StaticLimit.InvocationMode("Digits=20");
 t1 = new BigInteger(128, 24, r);
 assert StaticLimit.InvocationMode("Digits=20");
 t2 = new BigInteger(128, 24, r);
 assert StaticLimit.InvocationMode("Digits=40");
 this.crypto_key = t1.multiply(t2);
}
```

Figure 3. PERC Pico Constructor for TheMission

non-captive scoped objects that are allocated within a constructor are not simply placed in the same scope as the constructed object this is because the client code that invokes the constructor generally does not know about the internal behavior of a constructor, so it normally cannot calculate how large the corresponding scope would need to be.

In this sample code, the BigInteger.multiply() method is known to be declared with a @CallerAllocatedResult annotation. This indicates that the method places its result into a memory buffer that is supplied by the caller. The caller decides where the result is to be placed. It may not be in the caller's private scope. In this case, the result of the t1.multiply() invocation is placed in the constructed scope, so that it can be directly referenced by this object's crypto_key field.

Note that the constructor for TheMission is declared @StaticAnalyzable. This means that the compiler is expected to automatically analyze the sizes of the respective scopes[2]. For @StaticAnalyzable code, the PERC Pico compiler is also able to automatically compute the required size of the thread's run-time stack, including the stack of backing stores for private memory area scopes. The JSR-302, Annotated JSR-302, and C semantic models do not provide any support for analysis of thread stack sizes. With those models, stack size analysis must be performed by third-party tools or ad hoc techniques specific to each development effort.

There are two scopes that are relevant to this particular example: the private temporary memory scope of the constructor must hold one AbsoluteTime object, one Random object, and two BigInteger objects; the constructed scope of the constructor must hold the BigInteger object returned from t1.multiply(). The BigInteger data

---

2. Within @StaticAnalyzable methods, programmers are required to insert stylized assertions limiting the number of times loops iterate. The assertions may use symbolic values derived from static information available in a caller's context. The PERC Pico compiler rejects programs that are declared to be @StaticAnalyzable if the required iteration bounds are not specified. PERC Pico does not enforce that programmer-declared iteration bounds are correct, though testing application code with assertions enabled will throw an AssertionError if the programmer-declared iteration bounds are incorrect.

type represents arbitrary precision, so its memory requirements depend on the value to be represented. The documentation for the BigInteger constructor makes clear that the memory requirements can only be computed (for any given context) if the programmer supplies an assertion to bound the value to be stored within the constructed BigInteger object. This example shows that each of the invocations responsible for constructing or allocating a BigInteger object is preceded by an assertion that limits the number of digits required to represent the object in a decimal representation of the integer.

4. COMPARISONS BETWEEN PERC PICO AND JSR-302 ANNOTATIONS

There are fundamental differences between the approaches of PERC Pico and JSR-302. These differences are motivated by slightly different design objectives. Some of the key distinctions are highlighted in the following enumerated lists.

Rules for JSR-302 scopes. Based on source code annotations, the JSR-302 checker enforces the following invariant properties:

1. For classes that are annotated to reside only in particular scopes, assure that the class is instantiated only within the specific named scope.

2. In the case that a superclass has different annotations than its subclass, certain upcasts from the subclass to the superclass are forbidden.

3. Instance field annotations may indicate that the field always refers to the same scope as the object itself.

4. Instance field annotations may indicate that the field always refers to immortal memory, or to a specific named scope.

5. Certain instance field annotations may indicate that the field refers to an object in an unknown scope.

6. Certain method invocations require that certain reference arguments refer to the same scope as the object that is the target of the invocation.

7. Certain method invocations require that particular reference arguments refer to specific named scopes, or to immortal memory.

8. Certain method invocations allow particular reference arguments to refer to objects residing in unknown scopes.

Rules for PERC Pico scopes. In contrast, the invariants enforced by the PERC Pico verifier are the following:

1. Certain instance fields are known to refer to immortal memory.

2. Certain instance fields are known to refer to objects residing the same scope as this.

3. The remaining instance fields are known to refer to objects residing in immortal memory or to objects residing in any scope that encloses (is more outer-nested than) the scope of this.

4. Certain method invocations require that certain reference arguments refer to immortal memory.

5. Certain method invocations require that certain reference arguments refer to objects residing in the same scope as the object that is the target of the invocation.

6. Certain method invocations require that particular reference arguments refer to scopes that enclose (are more outer-nested than) the scope of the object that is the target of the invocation.

7. Certain method invocations allow particular reference arguments to refer to objects residing in unknown scopes.

While the JSR-302 checker has the ability to statically enforce the invariant properties that are relevant to the JSR-302 scope safety model, it does not gather the information required to enforce, for example, that particular unknown scopes are known to enclose (be more outer-nested than) or be the same as certain other unknown scopes. Likewise, the PERC Pico verifier does not keep track of the information required to enforce the JSR-302 model. For example, there is no notion of named scopes within PERC Pico, and there is no way for a PERC Pico programmer to describe a requirement that instances of a particular class may only be instantiated within particular scopes. Thus, there is no way to translate PERC Pico annotations into equivalent JSR-302 annotations, or to translate JSR-302 annotations into equivalent PERC Pico annotations.

Differences in allowed behaviors. The execution models of the PERC Pico and JSR-302 environments also differ significantly. The most noteworthy distinction is the respective treatments of scopes.

In PERC Pico, a scope is a hidden implementation artifact, similar to an activation frame in C or Ada. There is no PERC Pico API to allow application software to refer to a particular scope, or to ask how large it is, or to ask how much memory remains available within it. There is also no API to ask which scope holds a particular object, or to request that a particular new object allocation be taken from a particular scope. This is intentional. If application software were allowed to directly manipulate scopes, then static analysis of scope safety would be much more difficult.

In contrast, JSR-302, because it is structured as a literal subset of RTSJ, treats scopes as first-class objects. While this generality provides a certain expressive power to software developers, it also introduces difficult challenges for static analysis. For example, with JSR-302, any software component that has access to an object residing in a particular scope is allowed to create new objects in that same scope. The protocol is straightforward: (1) invoke area = MemoryArea.getMemoryArea(object), and (2) invoke area.executeInArea(logic) with a Runnable logic argument that performs memory allocations. Note that in the presence of such allocations, it is extremely difficult for a static analysis tool to automatically calculate the required size of each scope.

Another distinction between PERC Pico and JSR-302 execution models is that PERC Pico allows classes to be dynamically loaded into mission memory, whereas JSR-302 requires all classes to be loaded into immortal memory prior to initialization of the application. The static variables of a PERC Pico dynamically loaded class may refer to objects residing in outer-nested mission scopes, whereas JSR-302 assumes that static variables refer only to immortal memory.

PERC Pico enables a more concise and more abstract programming style. Early experimentation with PERC Pico in several different domains has confirmed that the abstractions it supports make it easier to develop and maintain complex and evolving software systems [14]. In the paragraphs that follow, we draw several comparisons between the Annotated JSR-302 and PERC Pico semantic models.

Guiding Design Principles. JSR-302 is implemented as a specialization of the RTSJ. The intended benefit of structuring the JSR-302 standard as a subset of full RTSJ is that JSR-302 application code, including reusable JSR-302 software modules, will run on any RTSJ implementation unchanged[3]. The simplicity of the JSR-302 annotation system was motivated in part by a desire to formally prove relevant attributes of the semantic model.

PERC Pico is structured instead as a specialization of standard edition Java. The higher levels of abstraction provided by this semantic model were motivated by a desire to ease the software development and maintenance burden with less emphasis on developing a formal proof of the semantic properties.

In theory, it is easier to qualify the tool chain of a JSR-302 implementation but easier to develop and maintain a PERC Pico application.

Scope Relationships. One of the strengths of PERC Pico is that the PERC Pico annotations assert relative rather than absolute scope nesting relationships. When describing the semantic constraints on a particular API, the PERC Pico programmer uses annotations to state that certain arguments must reside in scopes that surround, equal, or are enclosed by the scopes holding certain other arguments. This means that the same API can be used in many different contexts, as long as the actual arguments satisfy the constraints. In contrast, JSR-302 annotations specify that particular classes always reside in particular named scopes. If the same class is required to appear in multiple distinct scopes, programmers may be required to replicate the class (possibly using inheritance), and annotate each replication of the class with the distinct scope name in which it is intended to appear.

Scope Management. With Annotated JSR-302, classes that are not annotated are not allowed to escape the scope in which they are allocated. Classes that are annotated may be seen in other scopes, because the class annotation specifies the name of the scope in which all instances of that class reside. The JSR-302 annotation checker enforces that annotated classes are only instantiated when the current scope matches the named scope. The run-time environ-

ment's notion of current scope changes under explicit program control, with invocations of the ManagedMemory.enterPrivate-Memory() or MemoryArea.executeInArea() methods. With Annotated JSR-302, it is the responsibility of application code to calculate the size of each scope.

With PERC Pico, instances of any class may reside in any scope. PERC Pico annotations are associated with reference variables rather than the class declarations. Certain variables are known to refer to the current method's private scope. Other variables are known to refer to scopes that enclose (are either identical to, or externally nested around) certain other scopes. Scopes are entered and exited implicitly, as control flows into and out of methods. Scopes are sized automatically as guided by static analysis of the memory allocation needs associated with each scope.

Abstraction and Information Hiding. With Annotated JSR-302, it is generally not possible to accurately calculate the required sizes of each scope without having a full awareness of the memory allocation behavior that occurs inside of abstract data types. These implementation details are ideally hidden from users of the abstract data type because any dependency on this information makes code brittle. If subsequent software maintenance activities make changes to the internal memory allocation behaviors, it becomes necessary to find and update all of the code throughout the application that makes use of this information.

With PERC Pico, software developers have the option of structuring code so that a static analysis tool automatically computes the required sizes of each scope. If evolution of an application's source code results in changes to its internal memory allocation behavior, the static analysis tool automatically reflects these changes in all relevant scope sizes when the code is recompiled. Further, PERC Pico introduces the notion of a constructed scope. A *constructed scope* represents a conceptual expansion of the scope that holds a newly allocated this. This scope serves to hold the objects that are allocated within a constructor or within *reentrant scope* methods (such as Vector.add()) which must reside at the same (or enclosing) scope level as the constructed object because they must be referenced from the constructed object.

Reuse of Software Components and Certification Artifacts. It is difficult to reuse software and certification evidence with Annotated JSR-302 because classes must be annotated differently for each context (scope) in which they appear. This results in code replication (possibly using inheritance) rather than code sharing. Each replica of the code must be independently certified in its given context. Programming errors in the sizing of scopes for particular contexts may cause the software to fail in those contexts.

In contrast, the PERC Pico annotations allow the same code to be used in many different contexts with its memory usage automatically tailored for the context in which it appears.

Modular Composition of Software and Certification Evidence.

Both PERC Pico and annotated JSR-302 represent significant improvements over vanilla RTSJ in that annotations on component interfaces clarify the scope requirements associated with incoming arguments and instance fields. This allows the static checker to assure that composition of software components does not introduce scope assignment errors.

---

[3]. This is a theoretical benefit which is not yet demonstrated. The degree to which this objective can be satisfied is affected by the weaker semantics of particular RTSJ services. For example, RTSJ implementations may not support priority ceiling emulation. When deployed on an RTSJ implementation that does not support priority ceiling emulation, the RTSJ implementation is expected to emulate priority ceiling emulation using priority inheritance. Further, RTSJ as currently defined lacks services to avoid fragmentation of scope backing store memory. This means entry into and exit out of memory scopes is more expensive, less predictable (not deterministic) in execution time, and more vulnerable to failure due to memory fragmentation.

In the case that certification artifacts have been gathered for independent software components, it is easier to leverage these preexisting certification artifacts with PERC Pico than with Annotated JSR-302. This is because a PERC Pico software component can be integrated in many different contexts without any changes to the PERC Pico source or executable code. Further, the PERC Pico annotations assure more preconditions than the JSR-302 annotations, including availability of memory within relevant scopes and availability of backing store and stack memory to create additional scopes as might be required to reliably execute the code of a particular software component. One reason it is more difficult to reuse certification evidence gathered for Annotated JSR-302 software components is because Annotated JSR-302 components often need to be customized for use in different contexts. Among the certification artifacts that would be reused in an ideal scenario are audited logs of peer review activities, traceability of requirements to source to test plan, requirements-based test plan, and analysis of test results and code coverage

Design Patterns. The JSR-302 annotation system is designed primarily to support the scoped memory design pattern in which all objects of a linked data structure reside in the same scope. It handles this particular design pattern fairly well, without requiring annotations on class declarations. Whenever a given execution context refers to multiple distinct scopes (such as when computations use temporary objects to produce a result object result and the result object must be stored into a more permanent outer-nested structure), the JSR-302 annotation system becomes cumbersome. This is when it becomes necessary to name scopes and bind particular class instances to specific named scopes. Sometimes, it is possible to create multiple versions of a library class using inheritance, with each version bound to a distinct named scope. However, early experimentation with the JSR-302 annotation system suggests it is not always possible to achieve the desired flexibility by subclassing predefined standard libraries, and even when it is possible, the resulting code can be difficult to understand because of the requirement to divide logical control flows between multiple Runnable objects.

In contrast, the PERC Pico annotation system was designed with specific design patterns in mind, including differentiation between scoped and captive-scoped variables, constructed scopes, caller-allocated-result methods, reentrant-scope classes, and same-scope linked data structures. The annotations have evolved to improve the ease of expression for common design patterns during nearly five years of experimentation with a variety of applications, including implementation of scoped-memory collection libraries, a scoped-memory dynamic class loader, implementation of prototype interrupt-driven device drivers in Java, and several representative real-time applications.

5. CONCLUSIONS

While it is valuable to have a standard for safety-critical Java, it is also important to allow individual software development projects to select tools and methodologies that effectively address the specific requirements of that project. In the ideal, standard solutions enjoy the benefits of better documentation, greater availability of development tools and reusable software components from third parties, higher quality and lower cost software development tools

due to competitive market forces and larger economies of scale, and easier recruiting of competent developers already familiar with the standard from prior experience on other projects. However, when specifications created by committees are standardized without having proven their value in prior real-world deployments, it is much more difficult to realize these traditional benefits. The tutorial describes some of the benefits offered by certain alternative approaches to safety-critical development with the Java language.

6. ACKNOWLEDGEMENTS

The author owes special thanks to Ales Plsek, Daniel Tang, and Jan Vitek of Purdue University for their efforts in designing and implementing the JSR-302 annotation system, for countless discussions clarifying my understanding thereof, for providing me with early access to their implementation of the annotation checker for experimentation, and for helping me to implement representative code fragments. It is important to emphasize that the shortcomings of the JSR-302 annotation system discussed in this paper are primarily the result of constraints imposed by the JSR-302 expert group rather than the result of their design choices.

7. BIBLIOGRAPHY

[1] K. Arnold, J. Gosling, D. Holmes. *The Java™ Programming Language, 4th edition.* 928 pages. Prentice Hall PTR. Aug., 2005.

[2] K. Nilsen, *Differentiating Features of the PERC Virtual Machine,* http://www.atego.com/download-center/white-paper/differentiating-features-of-the-aonix-perc-virtual-machine/

[3] G. Bollella, B. Brosgol, J. Gosling, P. Dibble, S. Furr, M. Turnbull, *The Real-Time Specification for Java,* Addison Wesley Longman, 195 pages, Jan. 15, 2000.

[4] K. Nilsen, *Making Effective Use of the Real-Time Specification for Java,* Atego White Paper, September 2004, available at http://research.aonix.com/jsc/rtsj.issues.9-04.pdf.

[5] F. Pizlo, J. Fox, D. Holmes, J. Vitek, "Real-Time Java Scoped memory: design patterns and semantics", *Proceedings of the IEEE International Symposium on Object-Oriented Real-Time Distributed Computing (ISORC),* pp. 101-110. Vienna, Austria, May, 2004.

[6] J Consortium Inc. *International J Consortium Specification: Real-Time Core Extensions,* 2000.

[7] P. Puschner, G. Bernat, A. Wellings, "Making Java Real-Time", *The Annals of the Marie Curie Fellowship Association (MCFA),* vol. 2, pp. 76-81, Marie Curie Fellowship Association, 2003.

[8] J. Kwon, A. Wellings, S. King, "Ravenscar-Java: a High-Integrity Profile for Real-Time Java", *JGI '02 Proceedings of the 2002 joint ACM-ISCOPE Conference on Java Grande,* pp. 131-140, ACM New York, NY, USA, 2002.

[9] M. Schoeberl, H. Sondegaard, B. Thomsen, A. Ravn, "A Profile for Safety Critical Java", *ISORC '07 Proceedings of the 10th IEEE International Symposium on Real-Time Distributed Computing,* pp. 94-101, IEEE Computer Society Washington, DC, USA, 2007.

[10] *Meeting minutes, notes, and preliminary materials related to an early draft specification for safety-critical Java*, available at http://research.atego.com/jsc/index.html.

[11] *PERC Pico User Manual*, Apr. 19, 2008, available at http://research.atego.com/jsc/pico-manual.4-19-08.pdf.

[12] D. Locke, B. S. Andersen, B. Brosgol, M. Fulton, T. Henties, J. Hunt, J. Nielsen, K. Nilsen, M. Schoeberl, J. Tokar, J. Vitek, A. Wellings. *Safety-Critical Java Technology Specification, Public Draft*, version 0.78, Oct. 2010, available at http://www.jcp.org/en/jsr/detail?id=302.

[13] P. van der Linden. *Just Java 2, Sixth Edition.*816 pages. Sun Microsystems Press, Prentice Hall. 2004.

[14] M. Richard-Foy, T. Schoofs, E. Jenn, L. Gauthier, K. Nilsen. "Use of PERC Pico for Safety Critical Java", *Conference Proceedings: Embedded Real-Time Software and Systems*, Toulouse, France, May 2010.

[15] J. Durbin, R. Scharading. "The Modernization of the Aegis Fleet with Open Architecture", *Conference Proceedings System and Software Technology Conference*, Salt Lake City, UT, May 2011.

[16] K. Nilsen. "Improving Abstraction, Encapsulation, and Performance within Mixed-Mode Real-Time Java Applications." *Conference Proceedings of the ACM JTRES '07 5th International Workshop on Java Technologies for Real-Time and Embedded Systems*, Vienna, Austria, September, 2007.

Keynote Presentation:
Programming the Turing Machine

Barbara Liskov
Department of Electrical Engineering
and Computer Science
Massachusetts Institute of Technology
39 Vassar St.
Cambridge, Massachusetts 02139
liskov@csail.mit.edu

ABSTRACT

Turing provided the basis for modern computer science. However there is a huge gap between a Turing machine and the kinds of applications we use today. This gap is bridged by software, and designing and implementing large programs is a difficult task. The main way we have of keeping the complexity of software under control is to make use of abstraction and modularity. This talk will discuss how abstraction and modularity are used in the design of large programs, and how these concepts are supported in modern programming languages. It will also discuss what support is needed going forward.

Categories and Subject Descriptors

D.2.11 [**Software Architectures**]: Data abstraction, Information hiding;
D.3.3 [**Programming Languages**]: Language Constructs and Features – *abstract data types*

General Terms

Design, Reliability, Languages, Verification.

Keywords

Abstraction, Modularity, Programming Languages, Software Design

Program Proving Using Intermediate Verification Languages (IVLs) like Boogie and Why3

K. Rustan M. Leino
Microsoft Research
Redmond, WA, USA
leino@microsoft.com

ABSTRACT

A program verifier is a complex piece of software. To deal with this complexity, a standard architecture of a modern program verifier consists of two basic parts: a front end and a back end, separated by an *intermediate verification language (IVL)*. The separation of concerns obtained by this architecture is analogous to that in compilers: the front end is concerned with breaking down the semantics of given source-language programs into the more primitive operations of the intermediate language, and the back end is concerned with encoding the meaning of the intermediate program as efficient theorem-prover input.

Two prevalent IVLs today are Boogie 2 and Why3. In this invited talk, I will give a tour of the Boogie language. Through a set of examples, I will illustrate how a verifier may translate common source-program features into an IVL. A verification engine for the IVL is then applied to perform the actual verification. In this way, you can obtain a program verifier for your own language by building a new front end and reusing an existing verification engine.

Categories and Subject Descriptors

D.2.4 [**SOFTWARE ENGINEERING**]: Software/Program Verification—*Assertion checkers*

Keywords

Intermediate verification languages, verification tools, verifier architecture, formal verification, programming tools, auto-active verification, Boogie, Why3

1. REFERENCES

[1] M. Barnett, B.-Y. E. Chang, R. DeLine, B. Jacobs, and K. R. M. Leino. Boogie: A modular reusable verifier for object-oriented programs. In F. S. de Boer, M. M. Bonsangue, S. Graf, and W.-P. de Roever, editors, *Formal Methods for Components and Objects: 4th International Symposium, FMCO 2005*, volume 4111 of *Lecture Notes in Computer Science*, pages 364–387. Springer, Sept. 2006.

[2] F. Bobot, J.-C. Filliâtre, C. Marché, and A. Paskevich. Why3: Shepherd your herd of provers. In *BOOGIE 2011: First International Workshop on Intermediate Verification Languages*, Aug. 2011.

[3] J.-C. Filliâtre. Deductive program verification. Habilitation thesis, University Paris-Sud 11, Dec. 2011.

[4] J.-C. Filliâtre. Verifying two lines of C with Why3: an exercise in program verification. In R. Joshi, P. Müller, and A. Podelski, editors, *Verified Software: Theories, Tools, Experiments — 4th International Conference, VSTTE 2012*, volume 7152 of *Lecture Notes in Computer Science*, pages 83–97. Springer, Jan. 2012.

[5] J.-C. Filliâtre and C. Marché. The Why/Krakatoa/Caduceus platform for deductive program verification. In W. Damm and H. Hermanns, editors, *Computer Aided Verification, 19th International Conference, CAV 2007*, volume 4590 of *Lecture Notes in Computer Science*, pages 173–177. Springer, July 2007.

[6] C. Le Goues, K. R. M. Leino, and M. Moskal. The Boogie Verification Debugger (tool paper). In G. Barthe, A. Pardo, and G. Schneider, editors, *Software Engineering and Formal Methods - 9th International Conference, SEFM 2011*, volume 7041 of *Lecture Notes in Computer Science*, pages 407–414. Springer, Nov. 2011.

[7] K. R. M. Leino. Specification and verification of object-oriented software. In M. Broy, W. Sitou, and T. Hoare, editors, *Engineering Methods and Tools for Software Safety and Security*, volume 22 of *NATO Science for Peace and Security Series D: Information and Communication Security*, pages 231–266. IOS Press, 2009. Summer School Marktoberdorf 2008 lecture notes.

[8] K. R. M. Leino and M. Moskal. Usable auto-active verification. In T. Ball, L. Zuck, and N. Shankar, editors, *UV10 (Usable Verification) workshop*. http://fm.csl.sri.com/UV10/, Nov. 2010.

[9] K. R. M. Leino and P. Rümmer. A polymorphic intermediate verification language: Design and logical encoding. In J. Esparza and R. Majumdar, editors, *Tools and Algorithms for the Construction and Analysis of Systems, 16th International Conference, TACAS 2010*, volume 6015 of *Lecture Notes in Computer Science*, pages 312–327. Springer, Mar. 2010.

[10] K. R. M. Leino, J. B. Saxe, and R. Stata. Checking Java programs via guarded commands. In B. Jacobs, G. T. Leavens, P. Müller, and A. Poetzsch-Heffter, editors, *Formal Techniques for Java Programs*,

Technical Report 251. Fernuniversität Hagen, May 1999.

[11] K. R. M. Leino and W. Schulte. A verifying compiler for a multi-threaded object-oriented language. In M. Broy, J. Grünbauer, and T. Hoare, editors, *Software Safety and Security*, volume 9 of *NATO Science for Peace and Security Series D: Information and Communication Security*, pages 351–416. IOS Press, 2007. Summer School Marktoberdorf 2006 lecture notes.

Hi-Lite: The Convergence of Compiler Technology and Program Verification

Johannes Kanig
AdaCore
46 rue d'Amsterdam
Paris, France
kanig@adacore.com

Edmond Schonberg
AdaCore
104 Fifth Avenue
New York, NY
schonberg@adacore.com

Claire Dross
AdaCore
46 rue d'Amsterdam
Paris, France
dross@adacore.com

ABSTRACT

Formal program verification tools check that a program correctly implements its specification. Existing specification languages for well-known programming languages (Ada, C, Java, C#) have been developed independently from the programming language to which they apply. As a result, specifications are expressed separately from the code, typically as stylized comments, and the verification tools often bear no direct relation to the production compiler. We argue that this approach is problematic, and that the compiler and the verification tools should be integrated seamlessly. Based on our current work on the Hi-Lite project to develop a formal verification tool for Ada 2012, we show that in an integrated setting, the compiler becomes the centerpiece of the verification architecture, and supports both static proofs and run-time assertion checking. Such an environment does much to simplify software certification.

Categories and Subject Descriptors

F.3.1 [**Logics and Meaning of Programs**]: Specifying and Verifying and Reasoning about Programs—*Pre- and Postconditions, Mechanical Verification*; D.2.4 [**Software Engineering**]: Software/Program Verification—*Formal Methods, Programming by Contract*; D.3.4 [**Programming Languages**]: Processors—*Compilers*

Keywords

Compiler technology, formal verification, testing

1. INTRODUCTION

Most programming languages commonly used in embedded or critical software do not have suitable specification features for formal verification, such as pre- and postcondition for subprograms. Hence, such features end up being developed as independent specification languages for Ada [3], C [12, 8, 11], Java [6] and C# [4]. Since the compilers do not process these specifications, they are typically embedded in the source programs as special comments (SPARK, JML, E-ACSL), or as arguments to preprocessor directives that evaluate to the empty string (VCC, eCv). Only the authors of Spec# have extended the C# language with specifications and created a new compiler to handle code and specifications, different from the Microsoft production compiler, which causes some problems we discuss in Section 3. The verification tools understand specifications, and they can parse together the code and the specifications to create an annotated syntax tree for the program, on which proof machinery can operate.

A direct consequence of departing from the official language definition – by extending the language or by interpreting comments or arguments of preprocessing directives – is that the compiler and the verification tools cannot share the same frontend. Said otherwise, the existing compiler technology cannot be used directly as a frontend for these verification tools. There are also many reasons for not modifying an existing compiler to support these specifications: a compiler may not be readily available (the situation when SPARK was born) or modifying the internals of the compiler is considered too difficult (this is the reputation of gcc).

With the advent of Ada 2012, the latest version of the language, the situation is quite different, because contract features are now in the official language definition, so that any Ada 2012 compiler must support them. In this paper, we argue that not only *can* a compiler and formal verification share the same frontend, but they *should*. We discuss the advantages and disadvantages that this choice implies. We illustrate our case using the GNAT compiler and the verification tools GNATtest and GNATprove, which are developed in the context of the research project Hi-Lite [17].

In Section 2, we describe the new assertion mechanisms of Ada 2012, and we show how important it is that these assertions be built-in into the language, from a user point of view. In Section 3, we show how important this is for the tool developer, and we discuss in more detail the central role the compiler can play in a formal verification toolchain. In Section 4, we discuss related issues such as providing proved libraries and dealing with mathematical features in specifications.

2. EXECUTABLE ASSERTIONS AND CONTRACTS

The relationship between programming language design and correctness proof methodologies is an unsettled one. The pioneering articles of Floyd and Hoare use annotations that are added to existing code, without suggesting any particular relationship between the language of annotations and the surrounding programs. The methodology is aimed at manual proofs, and given the relative lack of abstractions in the programming languages of the time, the assertions are mostly arithmetic relations on integer values. Since then, all kinds of different logics (e.g. separation logic [22]) have been applied to all kinds of programming languages, such as C.

By contrast, the work of Dijkstra's school sees program development as evolving from pre/postconditions to code, and in fact in [13] most of the work consists in defining rigorously the logical formalism to use in the assertion language, and its relation to the eventual programs. However, there is no indication that authors envision some compilation machinery to relate assertions and code.

The development of Eiffel [1] takes a much more pragmatic approach. No doubt influenced by the slow progress in automated proof technologies, and the lack of enthusiasm on the part of the programming community for the rigors of Dijkstra's approach, Eiffel proposes that assertions about the behavior of code are (in addition to an expression of logical intent) optional run-time checks to be inserted in the code. As such, assertions and code are written in the same programming language. Meyer is also keenly aware that proof technology has matured sufficiently to be applied to contemporary software, and in [20] describes the use of Eiffel assertions in automated tools. A similar approach that combines formal verification and simulation applied to hardware design has been followed in the System Verilog community [24].

Ada 2012 follows the same two-pronged approach: the language offers a rich set of assertion mechanisms, where assertions are simply boolean expressions in Ada itself, that can be translated into run-time checks, and used profitably by automated tools to check whether these assertions are in fact obeyed by the code. The following hybrid approach then suggests itself: assertions that can be proved by static analysis can be removed from the code; those that can be proved to be false can be used to generate counterexamples; the remaining ones can generate run-time checks that will trigger an appropriate exception when violated.

To support a richer language of assertions, Ada 2012 incorporates a number of new expression forms, that allow a more functional style of programming than was the case for previous versions of the language.

2.1 New Expression Forms

Assertions can be used to specify the desired behavior of subprograms, loops, object creation routines, etc. In all these cases, the assertions are predicates, that is to say expressions that yield boolean values. To enrich the syntax of assertions, Ada 2012 offers several new boolean constructs. Some of them are familiar from other languages, and do not need much discussion: conditional expressions (if-expressions and case-expressions) and expression functions are similar to the constructs found in functional languages. Expression functions simplify immensely the introduction of abstractions in assertions.

Quantified expressions are familiar constructs in Logic, but are only rarely found in programming languages. They use familiar syntax:

```
for quantifier loop_parameter_specification
```

```
=> predicate
```

For example, the following expresses that array A is sorted:

```
for all I in A'Range =>
    I = A'Last or else A(I) <= A(I'Succ)
```

and the following states (inefficiently) that a number N is composite:

```
for some I in 2 .. N / 2 => N mod I = 0
```

It should be noted that quantified expressions are always expressed over a finite discrete range. It is up to the user to be careful no to choose a range that is too large and whose execution will take a very long time.

2.2 Contracts

Contracts specify the expected behavior of various language constructs. Even though the effect of any contract could be specified by using a single assertion mechanism, it is convenient to provide several varieties of contracts, depending on whether they apply to the behavior of subprograms or to properties of objects. In all cases, contracts are specified as *aspects* of entities. Aspects generalize the earlier Ada notion of attribute specification. Aspect specifications are attached directly to the declaration of the entity to which they apply.

2.2.1 Pre- and Postconditions

Predicates that express requirements on the input parameters of a function, and those that specify the characteristics of the result, are the most familiar. For example, a square root routine may be given the following declaration:

```
function Sqrt (X : Float) return Float
with
  Pre => X >= 0.0;
```

Postconditions often need to refer to the original value of an actual, and to the result of a function. The attributes 'Old and 'Result fulfill this need. We may add the following to our Sqrt routine:

```
function Sqrt (X : Float) return Float
with
  Pre  => X >= 0.0,
  Post =>
    ((Sqrt'Result) ** 2 <= X
    and then (Sqrt'Result + Epsilon) ** 2 > X);
```

where Epsilon is a constant declared elsewhere.

In a language with inheritance and polymorphism, we need to specify how the operations of a type T are inherited by extensions of T. In Ada 2012, the aspects Pre'Class and Post'Class of a subprogram P are inherited, *i.e.*, they also apply to an overriding of operation P on a descendant of T. These inheritance rules are consistent with the well-known Liskov substitution rules.

2.2.2 Type Invariants

In an imperative language with mutable objects, it is important to be able to define consistency conditions on an object of some composite type T. Whenever an object of this type is created or modified, we want to verify that the stated invariant is respected. However, if the type has visible components, some of which may be by-reference types, it is infeasible to verify that the invariant is respected after each potential modification. Therefore Ada 2012 chooses to allow invariants only on private (*i.e.*, opaque) types, in which case the invariant is typically expressed as a function call. The invariant must be checked whenever a type constructor is invoked, and whenever a subprogram that is visible to a client modifies an object of the type.

Here again inheritance and polymorphism require a separate mechanism to separate type-specific invariants from invariants that are intended to apply to all members of a class of types. The invariant `Type_Invariant'Class` indicates a property that all objects of a type descended from a given type must obey.

2.2.3 Subtype Predicates

In contrast with type invariants, subtype predicates typically apply to types with visible characteristics. Their simplest use is to provide for subsets of scalar types whose values are not contiguous. For example:

```
subtype Multiple is Natural with
  Dynamic_Predicate => Multiple mod 3 = 0;
```

If the bounds of a scalar subtype are static, and a `Static_Predicate` applies to it, the subtype can be used as the domain of iteration of a loop. On the other hand, if the bounds are non-static and the subtype has a `Dynamic_Predicate` defined, it cannot be used in a loop. If a subtype has a predicate of either kind, it cannot be used as the index of an array, and the attribute `'First`, `'Last`, or `'Range` cannot be applied to objects of the subtype. The subtype predicate is evaluated at places where a conversion to the subtype takes place: initialization, assignment, parameter passing.

2.3 The Advantages of Executable Contracts

The possibility of making assertions and contracts part of the executable benefits the programmer in two ways:

- it gives the programmer a gentle introduction to the use of contracts, and encourages him to develop assertions and code in parallel. This is natural when both are expressed in the same programming language.

- executable assertions can be enabled and checked at run time, and this gives valuable information to the user. When an assertion fails, it means that the code failed to obey desired properties (*i.e.*, the code is erroneous), or that the intent of the code has been incorrectly expressed (*i.e.*, the assertion is erroneous) – and experience shows that both situations arise equally often. In any case, the understanding of the code and properties of the programmer are improved. This also means that users get immediate benefits from writing additional assertions and contracts, which greatly encourages the adoption of contract-based programming.

- contracts can be written and dynamically verified even when the contracts or the program are too complex for automatic proof. This includes programs that explicitly manipulate pointers, for example.

Executable contracts can be less expressive, or more difficult to write, in some situations. This is discussed in Section 4.

In summary, Ada 2012 in itself enables contract-based, dynamic verification of complex properties of a program. GNATprove enables contract-based static deductive verification of a large subset of Ada 2012.

3. SHARING THE COMPILER FRONTEND

We have discussed in the introduction how, given the absence of annotations in some programming languages, program verification tools cannot use an existing compiler frontend for their syntactic and semantic analysis phase, and instead must develop their own parser/semantic analyzer for the language, enriched with a similar tool for the annotations. We also have indicated that the situation is different in a language whose definition includes annotations, such as Ada 2012. We use the GNAT frontend to parse and analyze Ada programs, and take the GNAT semantically analyzed syntax tree as input to the various verification tools we develop.

3.1 A Program Verifier as Backend of the Compiler

The first obvious advantage of using an existing frontend is that you do not have to write your own. Even for moderately complex languages such as C, this is a major undertaking[1], and for more complex ones such as Ada it is simply prohibitive. Complex issues such as scoping, overload resolution, generic instantiations, etc. have to be handled before any verification activities can proceed. It is clear that the workaround that consists in restricting the verification tool to a subset of the language, for which an independent frontend becomes feasible (as was done by Praxis for SPARK), is still a major investment. Note that GNATprove also applies to a subset of the full Ada 2012 language, which notably excludes pointers, exceptions and side effects in expressions (and contracts), but this subsetting is solely motivated by the limitations of the proof tools, and not because of frontend considerations.

Even disregarding the initial amount of work that has to be put in to obtain a parser and semantic analyzer for an existing language, this tool now must be maintained and updated when a new language version comes out, or when bugfixes have been applied to the original tool. The authors of the Spec# verifier have experienced this maintenance problem, which led them to adopt a different strategy for the design of Code Contracts [16]. They stress that deviating from the official language should be avoided so that standard tools can be used. To that end, they propose to encode contracts using existing language features, by calling methods of a special contract library. Similarly, JML tools regularly lag behind the evolution of the language, although recent efforts have been made to find solutions for

---

[1]You can find this quote from George Necula in the documentation of CIL:

> When I [...] started to write CIL I thought it was going to take two weeks. Exactly a year has passed since then and I am still fixing bugs in it. This gross underestimate was due to the fact that I thought parsing and making sense of C is simple. You probably think the same. What I did not expect was how many dark corners this language has [...].

that problem [9, 23]. SPARK shares the same problem, and is currently based on a subset of Ada 2005, instead of Ada 2012.

In summary, having contracts directly in the language, and using the compiler frontend as a basis for program verification tools not only saves the initial cost of building a separate frontend, but also decreases maintenance efforts involved in keeping such a tool up-to-date with the language and its compiler.

3.2 Which Program Representation Should be Used for Formal Verification?

Using directly a compiler frontend presents some problems of its own, even though they are relatively minor compared to the maintenance issues we previously discussed. A compiler is designed to translate programs to machine code, and not to do formal verification. Typically the compiler builds and decorates various abstract representations of the program, prior to generating an executable, and the question arises as to which of these representations is best suited as input to verification tools. Taking as an example the GNAT compiler, the work that is done in the Ada frontend can be described by three phases: parsing (building the tree from the source), semantic analysis (typing, name and overload resolution, enforcement of static semantics rules), and expansion (translation of higher-level constructs). The latter two phases are actually intertwined. Expansion is a first preparation phase for code generation, breaking down high-level features of Ada into simpler constructs, or replacing them by calls to the runtime library. For example the tasking features of Ada do need a whole supporting library, Ada 2012 quantified expressions are translated into loops, and generic subprograms and packages are instantiated by some complex macro-expansion. Some normalizing transformations are also done during expansion, such as filling in default parameters and reordering the actuals for subprogram calls.

The designer of a program verification tool needs to decide where in this chain he wants to branch off from the path that leads to code generation, and create the one that leads to static verification. In Hi-Lite, we target the Why3 [5] intermediate verification language. In some sense we *do* code generation, but the target language is sufficiently different that most of the GNAT expansion phase is of no use, and may be even harmful. For example, it is preferable to keep quantified expressions in their original form, because Why3 supports quantifiers directly in assertions, and even in programs there is a better way in Why3 to encode quantified expressions than by using loops. We do not entirely disable the expansion, though, because the normalizing steps of that phase, in particular the expansion of generics, are important and would be very costly to recreate.

3.3 Target- and Compiler-dependent Proofs

Program proofs in our toolchain depend on the target and the compiler that is used, in the sense that these proofs are not valid when either is changed. This fact sets our work apart from most program verification tools, and is directly related to the fact that the formal verification tool is implemented as a backend of the compiler. At first, this looks like a disadvantage, because proofs in other systems are supposed to depend only on the language definition, if such a thing exists – proved programs can then be used in

any context. In practice, however, it is difficult to pinpoint all places where the compiler is allowed to make choices or where the language behavior is undefined (see [15] for some striking examples in C), and for those places, the analysis tool can only be imprecise – because it cannot know what the compiler will choose. A typical example is the size of the machine integer types that are used for a program. To prove the absence of run-time errors (for example overflow on integer computations), a tool that is separate from the compiler will have to choose between:

- being incorrect, by assuming some fixed size which may or may not coincide with the actual compiler choice. This is of course not an option that tool builders will actually consider, but it may still occur, for example when the tool writer incorrectly uses the size of integers on the host on which the analysis is performed instead of their size on the target.

- relying on some mechanism (for example a configuration file) which contains the sizes a compiler is expected to choose for the given target platform. However, such a configuration file is rarely complete and must be kept up-to-date. As a consequence, this is a brittle approach. In this case, proofs are *not* platform-independent anymore.

By contrast, using the compiler as a base for the verification tool ensures the correctness of the tool's output because the machine integer size of the target is known to the compiler.

This consistency comes at the cost of giving up platform- and compiler-independent proofs. But in the safety-critical and embedded world, where Ada is used most, and where formal program verification is most useful, programs are generally platform-dependent, because they are mapped carefully onto the hardware, and issues of overflow are intrinsically target-dependent. Moreover, during the development of a safety-critical system, the compiler is rarely changed, as they often standardize on the behavior of a specific compiler version (with fixed compiler switches), in order to ensure binary size and run-time efficiency.

There *is* a potentially serious drawback of that approach: now *all* proofs are platform-dependent, even the proofs of components that are completely independent of such compiler choices. In particular libraries are often *designed* to be independent of the platform and compiler choices. However, if they are indeed independent, their correctness proof must be possible for any target, and establishing their correctness for a given target should amount to pushing a button, i.e. be fully automated.

One could argue that we verify neither the source code nor the object code, but some internal data structure of the compiler. While this is true, it is also true for any verification tool – it analyzes its internal tree, not the actual source file. The previous discussion has also shown that in many aspects, the tree that we analyze is closer to the actual object code than with other verification methods, while still sufficiently high-level to be amenable for formal proof.

3.4 Hybrid Verification

We have already seen in Section 2 that the existence of rich assertions in the language, and their support in the compiler, is crucial for the adoption of contract-based development. When these assertions are compiled and checked, for example during testing, developers get immediate benefit from writing this additional code. As these assertions are just boolean expressions in Ada 2012, no new syntax has to be learned. As we already stated, executing assertions is also a good way to find bugs in the assertions themselves. Assertions are not magically correct by construction, and experience shows that errors are evenly spread between the contracts and the code.

This interaction is the first step to an integration of test and proof, which is the main objective of the Hi-Lite project. We provide a tool GNATtest to do unit testing, which benefits from but does not require contracts and so-called testcase aspects. We also provide the formal verification tool GNATprove, for which the presence of contracts is mandatory[2], and which only supports a subset of Ada 2012. However, the essence of Hi-Lite is that GNATprove tolerates subprograms that do not fall into this subset; these subprograms must then be verified by testing.

It is not obvious that such a combination of testing and proof gives meaningful results, because both verification techniques are different. Testing has the advantage that no assumptions are made, except the sometimes quite bold assumption that the testing environment is sufficiently similar to the production environment. It has the disadvantage that relatively few guarantees can be given – namely only that the program behaves as specified in a limited number of situations. On the contrary, proof guarantees the correctness of the program in *all* situations, but only when its assumptions are met. For example, GNATprove assumes for each subprogram that its arguments are not aliased nor overlapping in memory, and that all variables have values allowed by their type. GNATprove checks these assumptions on all subprograms that fall in its supported subset, but not for others. There is a potential danger that proved functions are used in a context where these assumptions do not hold.

One of the key insights of Hi-Lite is that the combination of test and proof is meaningful when the assumptions of the proof tool are checked during testing [10]. We are again at a point where having control of the compiler hugely simplifies things. In a special mode that can be activated during testing, GNAT can insert additional dynamic checks for the assumptions of formal verification. For a compiler developer, this is a small amount of work, for an outside tool this amounts to much more work [7].

3.5 Reducing the Trusted Code Base

A drawback of our approach is that we have to trust not only the deductions of the verification tool, but also large parts of the compiler. There is much research on how to reduce this *trusted code base*. A possible approach is the so-called proof-carrying code (PCC) [21], where the compiler, possibly supported by user annotations, generates object code along with artifacts that allow to independently verify that the object code has certain properties. For example, proof-carrying code can certify the absence of certain classes of runtime errors, or the absence of certain security violations. These properties can now be checked by a small checker tool, and it does not matter anymore *how* the object code has been obtained. The compiler has been removed from the trusted code base.

Another approach is the *verified* compiler [19] (as opposed to the *verifying* compiler [18] approach illustrated by GNAT and GNATprove), where a compiler is implemented such that a machine-checkable proof certifies its correctness. Again, the compiler is not part of the trusted code base anymore, only the proof checker is.

We believe that the issue of the size of the trusted codebase is orthogonal to the issues described in this paper. Our compiler could very well generate proof-carrying code, and given sufficient man-power, we could very well formally prove the verification tool and the compiler, resulting in a "verified verifying compiler".

4. ENRICHING PROGRAMS AND SPECIFICATIONS

4.1 Providing Rich Libraries

It is commonly agreed that, for a programing language to be usable in practice, it must be supplied with good libraries. They allow the user to avoid rewriting standard pieces of code. They are less error prone and more efficient than what a typical user would write.

The same reasoning applies to their verification and formal proof. Libraries are more trustworthy (they have been verified) and they make the specification and the verification of programs that use them easier.

In Hi-Lite, special care has been taken to provide a library for containers well suited to proof [14]. Indeed, these data structures obviate the need for pointers, which are not easily handled in formal verification. What is more, specifications of functions on containers have been thoroughly written so that complex properties of client code can be checked.

4.2 More than Just Executable Semantics

Sometimes, executable assertions do not provide enough expressiveness, are a burden for the specification or make formal proof difficult. In such cases, it becomes necessary to enlarge the semantics of assertions.

4.2.1 *Mathematical Integers in Assertions*

One such case are assertions involving mathematical objects like integers. If the semantics of integer operations in assertions is the same as in the program, such operations in assertions may have to be guarded against overflow just as in program code, resulting in conditions that may be difficult to express. For example, if a programmer wants to be sure that the Ada expression `A + B` does not overflow, it is natural to write a precondition of the form `A + B in Integer`, which expresses that the result of the addition fits in the 32-bit integer type. However, the addition in this expression may itself overflow. Without giving more flexibility to the tools, the "solution" consists in writing a more complex expression with multiple cases depending on the sign of each argument, or introducing explicit conversions to a larger integer type. This burden may seem unnecessary for assertions designed to be checked by formal proof, since mathematical unbounded integers are easily handled in formal verification.

A solution to this problem is to introduce mathematical semantics for integer operations (i.e. arbitrary precision) that appear in assertions. In the absence of executable semantics, this is a natural choice, and is used for example in the B method [2]. However, it is at odds with our

[2]but GNATprove will fill in default contracts when none are given.

goal to provide the same semantics for execution and for proof. Therefore, this solution also implies the usage of a library for unbounded integers at execution time. Such a library, on the other hand, is a constraint not every safety critical software can afford (due to the possible run-time cost, unpredictable running time, possible dynamic allocation and finally the consequences for certification of the additional library). Also, choosing different semantics for assertions and programs (whether for execution or for proof) is a potential source of confusion. For example, asserting `A + B + C in Integer` in the precondition might not prevent `A + B + C` from overflowing inside the program, depending on the concrete values of the three variables and the chosen evaluation order.

Another partial solution, which is often sufficient, consists in using a larger machine integer type for intermediate results, instead of unbounded integers. For example, all four basic arithmetic operations on 32-bit integers can be done comfortably using 64-bit integers.

Since there does not seem to be a consensus on which semantics is the best for integer operations in assertion, we have decided to provide three alternative semantics in GNAT and GNATprove. The first one is the same semantics as in programs, where assertions have to be checked against overflows in their base type. The second one uses bigger machine integer types when needed, but will fail when the larger machine integer is still not big enough. The third one is the mathematical semantics that uses an arbitrary precision library. In the second and third cases, the compiler decides, using a simple static analysis, if a larger machine integer, or even an unbounded one, is needed.

It should be noted that the Ada standard does not require the compiler to issue an overflow error when an intermediate value does not fit into the base type. As long as the final result is correct, the intermediate computations can be carried out in any possible way. Of course, the standard disallows incorrect results due to overflows. We benefit from this liberty in the standard and have implemented the two "extended" semantics described above.

We believe that both semantics are also interesting for Ada programs, not just assertions. Therefore, all three types of semantics are available for assertions and for programs, and one can choose which one to use for which. Both the compiler and the proof tools support all three types of semantics, and agree on which is used when. Of course, the implementation was simplified greatly by the sharing of a common compiler frontend. A single piece of code takes the decision on what semantics to use for each arithmetic operation, and the compiler and the verification tool then act accordingly.

4.2.2 Proof-only Theories

For user-defined packages, executable assertions may also end up being insufficient. Some properties may well be impossible to express in the executable semantics (if they use mathematical real numbers for example), or the executable specification can be too complicated for the programmer, for the solver, or for both to handle. Some non-executable constructs, such as axioms, abstract (not completely defined) functions, variables or types *etc.*, could make the specification more user-readable or more efficient for formal verification.

For example, assume we want to define a function `Count`

that counts the occurrences of a given element in an array. The programmer can write an executable semantics for this function involving a recursive expression function that counts the occurrences of the element in a subrange of the array. Unfortunately, such a semantics may not allow the solver to easily deduce all needed properties, or at least not efficiently enough. Axioms or lemmas, describing the evolution of `Count` when an element is added or removed from an array for example, will make the solver's work easier.

In Hi-Lite, a Why3 [5] theory, usable only for proof, can be given for a package. This theory replaces the automatic translation of the package in the proof mechanism. Such a theory has been written for the container library for example. In future work, we plan to allow users to write these non-executable assertions directly in Ada. Indeed, that will make this mechanism usable for Ada programmers who do not know the Why3 formalism.

5. CONCLUSION

Even though many tools for formal program verification exist, very few of them have seen industrial acceptance, even when they address formal verification for an existing programming language in widespread use such as C. We believe that a necessary condition for easier adoption is the integration of the assertion language into the programming language; adoption is even smoother if both languages are essentially the same. Ada 2012 fulfills these requirements.

If this condition is met, the compiler becomes the central piece for the creation of safe software, because it understands the code and the assertion language, and can serve as a frontend for code generation, test and formal verification. This in turn makes it easier to realize and maintain tools for formal verification, that remain up-to-date in the face of advances in the language and in compiler technology. It also makes it possible to take into account platform-, compiler- and runtime-specific issues. The frontend for formal verification of the Hi-Lite project is built on top of the GNAT frontend.

Finally, we have shown that these choices are also compatible with expressing assertions in a way that is closer to a mathematical view. In Hi-Lite, we will provide a semantics of integer arithmetic for assertions that is closer to the mathematical view, and provide rich container libraries with high provability.

Acknowledgments. We would like to thank the many participants of the Hi-Lite mailing-list, in particular David Mentré, David Lesens and Stefan Lucks, as well as our colleagues and partners at AdaCore and Altran Praxis, for fruitful discussions that lead to some of the solutions presented here. We also want to thank the anonymous referees who raised some issues that are now discussed in the final version of this paper.

6. REFERENCES

[1] Eiffel : Analysis, design and programming language. Standard ECMA-367, 2d Edition (2006).

[2] J.-R. Abrial. *The B-book: assigning programs to meanings.* Cambridge University Press, New York, NY, USA, 1996.

[3] J. Barnes. *High Integrity Software: The SPARK Approach to Safety and Security.* Addison-Wesley

Longman Publishing Co., Inc., Boston, MA, USA, 2003.

[4] M. Barnett, K. R. M. Leino, and W. Schulte. The Spec# programming system: An overview. In G. Barthe, L. Burdy, M. Huisman, J.-L. Lanet, and T. Muntean, editors, *Construction and Analysis of Safe, Secure, and Interoperable Smart Devices*, volume 3362 of *Lecture Notes in Computer Science*, pages 49–69. Springer Berlin / Heidelberg, 2005.

[5] F. Bobot, J.-C. Filliâtre, A. Paskevich, and C. Marché. Why3: Shepherd your herd of provers. In *Proceedings of the First International Workshop on Intermediate Verification Languages, Boogie*, 2011.

[6] L. Burdy, Y. Cheon, D. R. Cok, M. D. Ernst, J. R. Kiniry, G. T. Leavens, K. R. M. Leino, and E. Poll. An overview of JML tools and applications. *International Journal on Software Tools for Technology Transfer (STTT)*, 7:212–232, 2005.

[7] M. Christakis, P. Müller, and V. Wüstholz. Collaborative verification and testing with explicit assumptions. In *Proceedings of the 18th International Symposium on Formal Methods*, Paris, France, August 2012.

[8] E. Cohen, M. Dahlweid, M. Hillebrand, D. Leinenbach, M. Moskal, T. Santen, W. Schulte, and S. Tobies. VCC: A practical system for verifying concurrent C. In *Proceedings of the 22nd International Conference on Theorem Proving in Higher Order Logics*, TPHOLs '09, pages 23–42, Berlin, Heidelberg, 2009. Springer-Verlag.

[9] D. R. Cok. OpenJML: JML for Java 7 by extending OpenJDK. In *Proceedings of the Third international conference on NASA Formal methods*, NFM'11, pages 472–479, Berlin, Heidelberg, 2011. Springer-Verlag.

[10] C. Comar, J. Kanig, and Y. Moy. Integrating formal program verification with testing. In *Proceedings of the Embedded Real Time Software and Systems conference*, ERTS² 2012, Feb. 2012.

[11] D. Crocker and J. Carlton. Verification of C programs using automated reasoning. In *Proceedings of the Fifth IEEE International Conference on Software Engineering and Formal Methods*, SEFM '07, pages 7–14, Washington, DC, USA, 2007. IEEE Computer Society.

[12] P. Cuoq, F. Kirchner, N. Kosmatov, V. Prevosto, J. Signoles, and B. Yakobowski. Frama-C, A software Analysis Perspective. In *Software Engineering and Formal Methods (SEFM)*, Oct. 2012. To appear.

[13] E. Dijsktra and C. Sholten. *Predicate Calculus and Program Semantics*. Springer, New York, Berlin, 1989.

[14] C. Dross, J.-C. Filliâtre, and Y. Moy. Correct code containing containers. In *5th International Conference on Tests & Proofs (TAP'11)*, Zurich, June 2011.

[15] C. Ellison and G. Rosu. An executable formal semantics of C with applications. In *Proceedings of the 39th annual ACM SIGPLAN-SIGACT symposium on Principles of programming languages*, POPL '12, pages 533–544, New York, NY, USA, 2012. ACM.

[16] M. Fahndrich, M. Barnett, D. Leijen, and F. Logozzo. Integrating a set of contract checking tools into Visual Studio. In *Proceedings of the 2012 Second International Workshop on Developing Tools as Plug-ins (TOPI 2012)*. IEEE, 2012.

[17] Hi-Lite: Simplifying the use of formal methods. http://www.open-do.org/projects/hi-lite/.

[18] C. A. R. Hoare. The verifying compiler, a grand challenge for computing research. In R. Cousot, editor, *VMCAI*, volume 3385 of *Lecture Notes in Computer Science*, pages 78–78. Springer, 2005.

[19] X. Leroy. A formally verified compiler back-end. *Journal of Automated Reasoning*, 43(4):363–446, 2009.

[20] B. Meyer. Eiffel as a framework for verification. In *Verified Software : Theories, Tools Experiments, Forst IFIP TC2/WG2.3 Conference*, Lecture Notes in Computer Science LNCS 4171. Springer, Zurich, Switzerland, 2005.

[21] G. C. Necula. Proof-carrying code. In P. Lee, F. Henglein, and N. D. Jones, editors, *POPL*, pages 106–119. ACM Press, 1997.

[22] J. C. Reynolds. An overview of separation logic. In B. Meyer and J. Woodcock, editors, *VSTTE*, volume 4171 of *Lecture Notes in Computer Science*, pages 460–469. Springer, 2005.

[23] Robby and P. Chalin. Preliminary design of a unified JML representation and software infrastructure. Technical report, SAnToS Laboratory, Kansas State University, 2009.

[24] C. Spear. *SystemVerilog for Verification: A Guide to Learning the Testbench Language Features*. Springer, New York, Berlin, 2008.

Implementation of a Simple Dimensionality Checking System in Ada 2012

Vincent Pucci
Adacore, Inc.
104 5th Avenue, NYC 10011
pucci@adacore.com

Edmond Schonberg
Adacore, Inc.
104 5th Avenue, NYC 10011
schonberg@adacore.com

ABSTRACT

We present the design and implementation of a dimensionality checking system in Ada 2012. The system is implemented in the GNAT compiler, and performs compile-time checks to verify the dimensional consistency of physical computations. The system allows the user to define his own system of units, and imposes no run-time changes nor multiple compilation passes on the user.

Keywords

Dimensionality Checking, System of units, Ada 2012

Categories and Subject Descriptors

D.3.3 [**Lnguage Constructs and Features**]: Data types and structures; D.3.4 [**Processors**]: Compilers

General Terms

Languages, Reliability
{keywordsAda2012, dimensionality checking, aspect specifications

1. INTRODUCTION

Dimensionality checking (DC) is a common practice in Physics and Engineering: formulae are checked to verify that meters are assigned to meters and not kilograms, that an empirical formula for viscosity yields a force per unit area, etc. From the earliest days of Ada and the introduction of derived types, there have been proposals to use the Ada type system to perform dimensionality checking as part of the static analysis of a program.

A comprehensive summary of the history of the problem is given in [1]. The naive approach consists in defining a new type for each dimensioned quantity, The type system will then reject dimension-incorrect assignments, but this approach leads to an unwieldy proliferation of multiplication operators for each pair of dimensioned quantities,

and becomes rapidly unworkable, Most sensible proposals involve discriminants for records that wrap a numeric quantity. These discriminants are either assumed to be stored apart from the record, or else the system requires two compilation passes, one with discriminants to perform the check, and one without them for actual execution.

Conceptually, all models (including ours) consist in associating some attribute (in general a vector of rational numbers) to existing types, and associating the required checks to arithmetic manipulations of such annotated types.

We have implemented in the GNAT compiler a simple DC system (dubbed GeoDesiC) that relies on the Aspect constructs of Ada 2012, and on some simple extensions to the semantic analyzer of the front-end of GNAT. The system allows the user to define his own system of units, and will verify that arithmetic operations that manipulate dimensioned quantities yield dimensionally consistent results.

We present an example MKS (for meter-kilogram-second) package and its use (see appendix, section 11). The MKS system of units is the international standard (SI) sytem of units based on seven base physical units: meter, kilogram, second, ampere, kelvin, mole and candela.

2. ADA 2012 ASPECTS FOR DIMENSIONAL CHECKING

2.1 Ada 2012 Aspects

Aspects constitute a new feature of the Ada 2012 language [2]. Aspects generalize earlier Ada notions of attributes, but present a number of advantages over them. Aspects are associated with the declaration of an entity and denote some specifiable characteristics of that entity. The aspects associated wih a given entity declaration are provided by an *Aspect_Specification* whose grammar is [2]:

```
with ASPECT_MARK [=> ASPECT_DEFINITION] {,
    ASPECT_MARK [=> ASPECT_DEFINITION] }

ASPECT_MARK ::= aspect_IDENTIFIER['Class]

ASPECT_DEFINITION ::= NAME | EXPRESSION | IDENTIFIER}
```

Aspect specifications can be provided for such familiar attributes as Size, Address, Convention, Inline, etc. They can also specify Ada 2012 characteristics such as Pre and Post-conditions, type invariants, etc. Finally, an implementation can provide additional aspects, for declarations that can legally receive them.

2.2 Aspects for Dimensional Checking

We introduce two implementation-defined aspects: **Dimension_System** and **Dimension**.

2.2.1 *Aspect Dimension_System*

The form of an aspect Dimension_System is as follows:

```
with Dimension_System => (
     DIMENSION, DIMENSION {, DIMENSION} );

DIMENSION ::= (
  [Unit_Name   =>] IDENTIFIER,
  [Unit_Symbol =>] SYMBOL,
  [Dim_Symbol  =>] SYMBOL)

SYMBOL ::= STRING_LITERAL | CHARACTER_LITERAL
```

An aspect Dimension_System can only be apploed to a numeric type, typically a floating point type of the appropriate precision (any numeric type can be used as a base). The aspect specifies the unit names, the unit symbols and the dimension symbols to be used when performing formatted output on dimensioned quantities. The aspect value is thus an aggregate of some internal array type. In an SI system, this aggregate will have seven components, but this is not required by GeoDesiC (the user can specify fewer or more physical dimensions).

Illustration of the syntax

```
    type Simple_Mks_Type is
        new Long_Long_Float
    with
    Dimension_System => (
      (Unit_Name => Meter,
          Unit_Symbol => 'm',
          Dim_Symbol => 'L'),
      (Unit_Name => Kilogram,
          Unit_Symbol => "kg",
          Dim_Symbol => 'M'),
      (Unit_Name => Second,
          Unit_Symbol => 's',
          Dim_Symbol => 'T')));
```

A type (more accurately a first subtype) to which the aspect Dimension_System applies is a *dimensioned type*.

2.2.2 *Aspect Dimension*

The form of an aspect Dimension is as follow:

```
with Dimension => (
  [[Symbol =>] SYMBOL,]
     DIMENSION_VALUE {,DIMENSION_VALUE} );

SYMBOL ::= STRING_LITERAL | CHARACTER_LITERAL

DIMENSION_VALUE ::=
    RATIONAL
  | others => RATIONAL
  | DISCRETE_CHOICE_LIST => RATIONAL

RATIONAL ::= [-] NUMERAL [/NUMERAL]
```

An aspect Dimension applies only to a subtype of a dimensioned type. The aspect specifies a string name (or charac-

ter literal) to be used for output [1], and the rational numbers that determine the dimensions of the physical entity represented by the subtype:

Illustration of the syntax

```
    subtype Frequency is Mks_Type
      with
      Dimension => (Symbol => "Hz",
        Second => -1,
        others => 0);
```

A subtype to which the aspect Dimension applies is a *dimensioned subtype*.

3. DESIGN CONSTRAINTS

GeoDesiC is a compile-time system: it does not modify run-time structures and must be able to perform dimensional checking on all numeric expressions. This imposes on the user the requirement that all variables and constants be of a dimensioned subtype. Constants whose type declaration lacks an aspect Dimension or whose initial expression is not dimensioned, as well as named numbers, are treated as dimensionless quantities.

- A special programming obligation applies to exponentiation: the exponent must be a dimensionless static rational constant, otherwise the base must be dimensionless and then the result is dimensionless as well. This is consistent with practice in Physics : variable exponents do not appear in formulae, unless the base of the exponentiation is dimensionless. (Variable exponents show up in geometric formulae, e.g. in characteristics of objects in n-dimensional space, but these are invariably dimensionless). Exponents in general must be rational numbers, not just signed integers. Fractional exponents are common in physical computations (e.g. the period of a pendulum as a function of length). Arithmetic computations on rationals are exact, which is a requirement for proper dimensionality checking. Thus, a rational arithmetic package is provided in GNAT for GeoDesiC use.

- Because of its frequent appearance in physical formulae, the square root function (defined in Ada.Numerics.Elementary_Functions) is recognized by GeoDesiC, and treated specially, so the dimensions of the result can be set to half the dimensions of the operand.

Example of the Square root function in GeoDesiC:

```
    subtype Area is Mks_Type
      with
      Dimension => ("m**2",
        Meter => 2,
        others => 0);

    A : constant Area := 2.0;
    L : Length;
    begin
      L := Sqrt (A);
```

---

[1]Note that the string here is optional. When not present, a special treatment is performed by GeoDesiC for output facilities (section 5).

- All the other predefined elementary functions are also recognized, and GeoDesic ensures that any parameters for these functions, as well as their results, are dimensionless. (There have been suggestions to support trignometric functions with radian as well as degree arguments).

  Example of improper use of Sin function in GeoDesiC:

  ```
  A : constant Area := 2.0;
  R : Mks_Type;
  begin
      R := Sin (A);
  ```

  The incorrect call to Sin is rejected with the following diagnostic:

  ```
  parameter of "Sin" must be dimensionless
  parameter has dimension [L**2]
  ```

4. IMPLEMENTATION

Arithmetic operations, assignment, object declarations with initialization expressions (component declarations with default expressions), exponentiation, function calls and return statements are operations that verify and/or compute the dimension vectors of the constituents of the operation at compile-time. (each one of the examples used below is followed by the corresponding compilation error messages).

- For addition operators, both operands must have the same dimension. Unary operations propagate the dimension of their operand.

  ```
  Result : Mks_Type;
  begin
      Result := cm + kg;
  ```

  Such an Incorrect addition is rejected with the following diagnostic:

  ```
  both operands for operation "+" must have
      same dimensions
  left operand has dimension [L]
  right operand has dimension [M]
  ```

- For multiplication operators (* and /) the operands are unconstrained, and the components of the resulting dimension vector are the sum (resp. the difference) of the component dimensions of the operands.

- For assignment the dimension vectors of name and expression must agree. A similar rule applies to parameter passing in calls.

  ```
  Result : Mks_Type;
  begin
      Result := cm * kg;
  ```

  Incorrect assignment is rejected with the following diagnoses:

  ```
  dimensions mismatch in assignment
  left-hand side is dimensionless
  right-hand side has dimension [L.M]
  ```

- For object declarations with initialization expressions, both the expression and the type mark must have the same dimensions, unless the expression is a literal.

  ```
  Correct_1 : constant Length := 2.0;
  Correct_2 : constant Length := 2.0 * m;
  Wrong     : constant Length := 2.0 * kg;
  ```

  Incorrect object declaration is rejected with the following diagnoses:

  ```
  dimensions mismatch in object declaration
  object type has dimension [L]
  object expression has dimension [M]
  ```

- For exponentiation, the exponent must be a static rational constant. The components of the resulting dimension vector are obtained by multiplying the corresponding components of the dimensions of the base by the value of the exponent.

- Both operands in a relational operation must have the same dimensions.

  ```
  Result : Boolean;
  begin
      Result := kg**(5/6) >= kg;
  ```

  An incorrect relational operation is rejected with the following diagnoses:

  ```
  both operands for operation ">=" must have
      same dimensions
  left operand has dimension [M**(5/6)]
  right operand has dimension [M]
  ```

- For functions (except elementary functions, see section 3), the resulting dimension vector is the dimension vector of the type entity.

- For return statements, the returned expression and return type must have the same dimensions. The following bodies display the outcome of such checks:

  ```
  Result : Time;

  function Correct (L : Length)
      return Time is
  begin
      return L * s / m;
  end Correct;

  function Wrong (X : Mks_Type)
      return Length is
  begin
      return X * kg;  -- Not a length
  end Wrong;

  begin
      Result := Correct (cm);

  -- Both Result and Correct (cm) denote
  -- a time value.
  ```

The incorrect return statement is rejected with the following diagnostic:

```
dimensions mismatch in return statement
returned type has dimension [L]
returned expression has dimension [M]
```

The modifications to the GNAT semantic analyzer are straight-forward; they rely on the existing Ada 2012 machinery for aspect specifications, and the details need not be discussed here. The interested reader will find them in the GNAT sources.

5. INPUT-OUTPUT

The current system provides formatted output, thanks to two generic packages for integer and float dimensioned types. If the argument of the output routine is a variable and if a symbol is provided in the dimension Aspect of its subtype declaration, then the symbol string is used as a suffix to the value. Otherwise the dimension vector is output in standard notation, e.g. *"m*kg*s** (-2)"*. Engineering conventions differ in the display of negative values for dimensions, and some may prefer to see *"m*kg/s**2"*.

Similarly to the elementary functions, GeoDesiC recognizes the put routines for dimensioned types, so it can output the dimension symbols as a suffix of the value.

6. MULTIPLE SYSTEMS OF UNITS

The user can declare different unit systems (cgs, British, etc.) following the model of the MKS package described in the appendix. Given that each dimensioned type is a distinct numeric type, any attempt to mix systems of units in a computation will be rejected statically. The user can also declare conversion functions between different systems, for which Ada 2012 expression functions provide a compact form:

```
function inches_to_mm (X : British_Type)
    return MKS_Type is (MKS_Type(2.54 * X));
```

However, such conversions lose track of the fact that both units denote a physical Length, so the checking in the presence of such conversions is not completely fool-proof.

7. EXAMPLES

This section illustrates two well-known simple physical systems, and presents dimensioned programs to compute their properties.

7.1 The simple pendulum

In this section, a simple example is used in order to illustrate the syntax of GeoDesiC.

7.1.1 Question:

Determine the length l of a simple pendulum (figure 1) whose period T_o equals 2 seconds (consider the case of small amplitude oscillations).
Data: $g = 9.81 ms^{-2}$ on Earth
Gravity on the surface of the Moon: one sixth of Earth's.

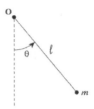

Figure 1: Pendulum oscillation

7.1.2 Solution:

$$T_o = 2\pi\sqrt{\frac{l}{g}} \qquad (1)$$

From equation 1, we deduce the expression of l:

$$l = \frac{gT_o^2}{4\pi^2} \qquad (2)$$

```
with Ada.Text_IO;            use Ada.Text_IO;
with System.Dim.Mks;         use System.Dim.Mks;
with System.Dim.Mks_IO;      use System.Dim.Mks_IO;
    --  provides Mks output routines

procedure Pendulum is
    --  Dimensioned subtype for gravitational
    --  constant on different bodies

    subtype Gravity is Mks_Type
      with
        Dimension => ("m.s**(-2)",
          Meter  => 1,
          Second => -2,
          others => 0);

    --  Data

    g   : constant Gravity := 9.81;
    --  on Earth

    gm  : constant Gravity := g / 6.0 ;
        --  on the surface of the moon

    T_0 : constant Time := 2.0;
    L   : Length;

begin
    L := g * T_0**2 / (4.0 * Pi**2);

    --  Output dimensioned results

    Put ("L_=_");
    Put (L, 1, 3, 0); New_Line;
    Put ("On_the_Moon,_L_=_");
    Put ((gm * T_0**2 / (4.0 * Pi**2)), 1, 3, 0);
end Pendulum;
```

7.1.3 Result:

```
l = 0.994 m
On the Moon, L = 0.166 m
```

38

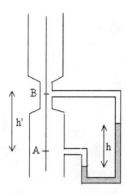

Figure 2: Venturi

7.2 The Venturi effect in constricted flow

This common fluid statics problem is a more ellaborate example and deals with various dimensioned formulae.

7.2.1 Questions:

- Determine the expression of the water flow in the Venturi Q_V (figure 2) in terms of pressure difference between points A and B and of the distance h'. Consider the perfect fluid case. Shaded part of device holds mercury (Hg)

- Evaluate the flow knowing that diameters of the neck and of the pipe are respectively 15 and 30 cm.

- Calculate both water average speeds v_A and v_B.

Data: $h = 75.0 cm$ and mercury density $\nu_{Hg} = 13.6$.

7.2.2 Solution:

- Flow conservation law and Bernouilli's theorem set:

$$v_B = v_A \frac{D^2}{d^2} \qquad (3)$$

$$\frac{1}{2} v_A^2 + \frac{p_A}{\nu_{H_2O}} + g \cdot z_A = \frac{1}{2} v_B^2 + \frac{p_B}{\nu_{H_2O}} + g \cdot z_B \qquad (4)$$

Equation 3 yields:

$$v_B^2 - v_A^2 = v_B^2 \left(1 - \beta^4 \right) \qquad (5)$$

where $\beta = \frac{d}{D}$.

And equation 4 leads to:

$$v_B^2 - v_A^2 = 2 \frac{p_A - p_B}{\nu_{H_2O}} - 2 \cdot g \cdot h' \qquad (6)$$

where $h' = z_A - z_B$

Hence, knowing that $Q_V = v_B S_B$ (where $S_B = \pi \frac{d^2}{4}$ is the venturi internal area at point B):

$$Q_V = \pi \frac{d^2}{4} \sqrt{\frac{2 \left(p_A - p_B \right) / \nu_{H_2O} - 2 \cdot g \cdot h'}{1 - \beta^4}} \qquad (7)$$

- In order to evaluate the flow, we introduce points 1 and 2 setting: $z_2 - z_1 = h$. By definition:

$$\begin{aligned} p_1 - p_2 &= \nu_{Hg} \cdot g \left(z_2 - z_1 \right) \\ &= \nu_{Hg} \cdot g \cdot h \\ &= p_A + \nu_{H_2O} \cdot g \left(z_A - z_1 \right) \\ -p_B - \nu_{H_2O} \cdot g \left(z_B - z_2 \right) & \qquad (8) \end{aligned}$$

Thus:

$$p_A - p_B = \left(\nu_{Hg} - \nu_{H_2O} \right) g \cdot h + \nu_{H_2O} \cdot g \cdot h' \qquad (9)$$

Replacing expression 9 in equation 6:

$$v_B^2 - v_A^2 = 2 \frac{\left(\nu_{Hg} - \nu_{H_2O} \right) g \cdot h}{\nu_{H_2O}} \qquad (10)$$

Finally, we deduce the new expression of Q_V:

$$Q_V = \pi \frac{d^2}{4} \sqrt{\frac{2 \left(\nu_{Hg} - \nu H_2 O \right) g \cdot h}{\nu_{H_2O} \left(1 - \beta^4 \right)}} \qquad (11)$$

The dimensioned program is as follows (for brevity we omit a separate subtype declaration for density):

```ada
with Ada.Text_IO;        use Ada.Text_IO;
with System.Dim.Mks;     use System.Dim.Mks;
with System.Dim.Mks_IO;  use System.Dim.Mks_IO;

procedure Venturi is
  --  Dimensioned subtypes

  subtype Area is Mks_Type
     with
       Dimension => ( Meter =>   2,
         others => 0);
  subtype Flow is Mks_Type
     with
       Dimension => ( Meter =>   3,
         Second => -1,
         others => 0);
  subtype Gravity is Mks_Type
     with
       Dimension => ( Meter =>   1,
         Second => -2,
         others => 0);
  subtype Speed is Mks_Type
     with
       Dimension => ( Meter =>   1,
         Second => -1,
         others => 0);

  --  Physical constants

  d_1    : constant Length := 15.0 * cm;
  d_2    : constant Length := 30.0 * cm;
  beta   : constant Mks_Type := d_1 / d_2;
  g      : constant Gravity := 9.81;
  h      : constant Length := 75.0 * cm;
  nu_Hg  : constant Mks_Type := 13.6;
  nu_H2O : constant Mks_Type := 1.0;

  Q_v    : Flow;
  S_B    : Area;
  v_A    : Speed;
```

```
v_B      : Speed;
```

begin
```
    —    Evaluation  of  Q_v

    S_B  :=  Pi  *  (d_1  /  2.0)**2;
    Q_v  :=  S_B  *
            (2.0  *  (nu_Hg  −  nu_H2O)  *  g  *  h  /
            (nu_H2O  *  (1.0  −  beta**4)))**(1/2);

    —    Exponent  1/2  can  be  used  instead  of  Sqrt
    —    (same  behavior  for  dimensioned  operand)

    Put  ("Q_v_=_");
    Put  (Q_v,  0,  3,  0);
    New_Line;

    v_B  :=  Q_v  /  S_B;
    v_A  :=  beta  *  v_B;

    —    Output  v_A  and  v_B
    Put  ("v_A_=_");
    Put  (v_A,  1,  2,  0);
    New_Line;

    Put  ("v_B_=_");
    Put  (v_B,  2,  1,  0);
end Venturi;
```

7.2.3 Results:

```
Q_v = 0.249 m**3.s**(−1)
v_A = 7.03 m.s**(−1)
v_B = 14.1 m.s**(−1)
```

8. CONCLUSIONS

Apart from the use of Ada 2012 features (which could even be transformed into Ada 2005 pragmas) and its full compile-time behavior, GeoDesiC makes no claims on originality, and is close in spirit to previous DC proposals for Ada. A dimension aspect is simply a set of discriminants stored away from a discriminated value. This allows the implementation to share discriminant vectors during semantic analysis, and garbage-collect them when analysis is complete. A substantial part of the implementation (trivial from an algorithmic point of view, but vital for usability) deals with output of dimensioned quantities. We hope that the relative ease of use of the system will make it attractive in Physics and Engineering applications, and we welcome feedback and suggestions for improvement from users.

Related work

The work of Christof Grein on the topic has been invaluable to us, and we have freely borrowed from the work described in [3], including the manipulation of rational and integer constants. The earliest proposal for dimensionality checking in Ada is due to Paul Hilfinger [4].

The Units of Measure technique in F# described in [5] has also been a source of inspiration to us, as well as the implementation of DC in Parasail (T.Taft, private communication). F# offers similar capabilities to the ones we describe, but in the context of a functional language with type inference. Thus much of the declarative machinery that Ada requires can be elided.

We hope that our simple model will finally make dimensionality checking widespread in scientific programming.

9. ACKNOWLEDGEMENTS

Many thanks are due to Hirstian Kirchev, Thomas Quinot, Bob Duff, Tucker Taft and Yannick Moy for numerous comments and productive discussions. We also thank the reviewers for several judicious suggestions.

10. REFERENCES

[1] C. Grein, D.A Kazakov, and Fraser Wilson: A survey of Physical Units Handling Techniques in Ada. Ada-Europe 2003, LNCS Vol. 2655, p.258-270. Springer, Heidelberg (2003)

[2] Ada Reference Manual, 13.3.1 Aspect Specifications. (2011) http://www.ada-auth.org/standards/12rm/html/RM-13-3-1.html

[3] C.Grein: Handling Physical Dimensions in Ada. (28 April 2008) http://www.christ-usch-grein.homepage.t-online.de/Ada/Dimension.html

[4] Paul N. Hilfinger: An Ada package for dimensional analysis. ACM Transactions on Programming Languages, 10, 2 (189-203) (Aprll 1988)

[5] Microsoft Developer Network, Units of Measure (F#). (May 2010) http://msdn.microsoft.com/en-us/library/dd233243.aspx

11. APPENDIX: THE MKS PACKAGE

GJAT provides a predefined MKS package with the following outline:

```
package System.Dim.Mks is
    —    Dimensioned  type  Mks_Type  with  7  units

    type Mks_Type is new Long_Long_Float
      with
        Dimension_System => (
          (Unit_Name   => Meter,
            Unit_Symbol => 'm',
            Dim_Symbol  => 'L'),
          (Unit_Name   => Kilogram,
            Unit_Symbol => "kg",
            Dim_Symbol  => 'M'),
          (Unit_Name   => Second,
            Unit_Symbol => 's',
            Dim_Symbol  => 'T'),
          (Unit_Name   => Ampere,
            Unit_Symbol => 'A',
            Dim_Symbol  => 'I'),
          (Unit_Name   => Kelvin,
            Unit_Symbol => 'K',
            Dim_Symbol  => "ÎŸ"),
          (Unit_Name   => Mole,
            Unit_Symbol => "mol",
            Dim_Symbol  => 'N'),
          (Unit_Name   => Candela,
            Unit_Symbol => "cd",
            Dim_Symbol  => 'J'));
```

```
subtype Length is Mks_Type
  with Dimension =>
    (Symbol => 'm', Meter => 1,
      others => 0);
subtype Mass is Mks_Type
  with Dimension =>
    (Symbol => "kg", Kilogram => 1,
      others =>    0);
subtype Time is Mks_Type
  with Dimension =>
    (Symbol => 's', Second => 1,
      others => 0);
subtype Electric_Current is Mks_Type
  with Dimension =>
    (Symbol => 'A', Ampere => 1,
      others => 0);
subtype Thermodynamic_Temperature
  is Mks_Type
  with Dimension =>
    (Symbol => 'K', Kelvin => 1,
      others => 0);
subtype Amount_Of_Substance is Mks_Type
  with Dimension =>
    (Symbol => "mol", Mole =>    1,
      others => 0);
subtype Luminous_Intensity is Mks_Type
  with Dimension =>
    (Symbol => "cd", Candela => 1,
      others =>    0);
```

— *SI Base units*

```
m    : constant Length                := 1.0;
kg   : constant Mass                  := 1.0;
s    : constant Time                  := 1.0;
A    : constant Electric_Current := 1.0;
K    : constant Thermodynamic_Temperature
                                       := 1.0;
mol  : constant Amount_Of_Substance
                                       := 1.0;
cd   : constant Luminous_Intensity
                                       := 1.0;
```

— *SI common prefixes for Meter*

```
um   : constant Length := 1.0E−06;   — micro
mm   : constant Length := 1.0E−03;   — milli
cm   : constant Length := 1.0E−02;   — centi
dm   : constant Length := 1.0E−01;   — deci
dam  : constant Length := 1.0E+01;   — deka
hm   : constant Length := 1.0E+02;   — hecto
km   : constant Length := 1.0E+03;   — kilo
Mem  : constant Length := 1.0E+06;   — mega
```

— *Similar SI prefixes for Kilogram, Second,*
— *and other units*
...

— *SI Derived dimensioned subtypes*

```
subtype Angle is Mks_Type
  with Dimension =>
    (Symbol => "rad", others => 0);
subtype Solid_Angle is Mks_Type
  with Dimension =>
    (Symbol => "sr", others => 0);
subtype Frequency is Mks_Type
  with Dimension =>
    (Symbol => "Hz", Second => −1,
      others => 0);
subtype Force is Mks_Type
  with
    Dimension =>
    (Symbol => 'N',
      Meter => 1, Kilogram => 1,
      Second => −2,
        others =>    0);
```
— *etc*

— *SI derived units*

```
rad : constant Angle        := 1.0;
sr  : constant Solid_Angle  := 1.0;
Hz  : constant Frequency    := 1.0;
N   : constant Force        := 1.0;
```
— *etc*
```
end System.Dim.Mks;
```

A New Robust and Efficient Implementation of Controlled Types in the GNAT Compiler

Hristian Kirtchev
AdaCore Technologies Inc.
104 5th Avenue, 15th Floor
New York, NY 10011, USA
kirtchev@adacore.com

ABSTRACT

This paper discusses a new implementation model for supporting Ada controlled types in the GNAT compiler [2]. After reviewing the semantics of controlled types, we revisit the original implementation from 1995 and discuss its performance issues. We then describe a new model which addresses all existing limitations and is shown to be superior to its predecessor. Finally, we conclude the paper with the status of the new implementation and possible future enhancements.

Categories and Subject Descriptors

D.2.7 [**Distribution, Maintenance, and Enhancement**]: Enhancement; D.2.8 [**Metrics**]: Performance measures; D.2.10 [**Design**]: Methodologies; D.3.4 [**Processors**]: Compilers

General Terms

Design, Languages, Performance

Keywords

controlled types, implementation, GNAT compiler

1. INTRODUCTION

The Ada programming language [3] defines a special class of types that offer direct control over the creation, update and destruction of an object. These types are referred to as "controlled types" and their structure is outlined in package `Ada.Finalization` (Fig. 1):

By default, the three routines `Initialize`, `Adjust` and `Finalize` have no effect. Types derived from `Controlled` or `Limited_Controlled` may override one or all of these procedures and specify desired behavior.

For each of the three possible actions, the language mandates the following semantic rules:

* Initialization - `Initialize` must be invoked after default initialization of an object has been carried out. This

```
type Controlled is abstract tagged private;
procedure Initialize (Object : in out Controlled);
procedure Adjust (Object : in out Controlled);
procedure Finalize (Object : in out Controlled);

type Limited_Controlled is
            abstract tagged limited private;
procedure Initialize
            (Object : in out Limited_Controlled);
procedure Finalize
            (Object : in out Limited_Controlled);
```

Figure 1: Excerpt from package Ada.Finalization

allows the user to open a database connection, create files or do any other kind of preliminary setup. Initialization of multiple controlled objects must be carried out in order of declarations.

* Finalization - `Finalize` must be invoked when an object or an access-to-controlled type is about to go out of scope. This usually happens when a stack frame is removed or a master is completed. Finalization permits all sorts of clean up actions to be carried out - deallocation of complex structures, closing of sockets, etc. Finalization of multiple controlled objects must be carried out in reverse order of declarations.

* Adjustment - `Adjust` must be called after the assignment of one object to another. `Adjust` is handy when replicating complex data structures that may require a deep copy.

2. THE 1995 IMPLEMENTATION OF CONTROLLED TYPES

The 1995 implementation (henceforth referred to as "the 95 implementation") [1] was first introduced in the early 90s and continued to be in use until 2012.

The basic approach of the 95 implementation is to treat controlled objects and their components as tree-like structures. These linked abstractions preserve the order of declaration and level of component nesting. Runtime support then walks the trees and performs adjustment and finalization actions.

To achieve this effect, types `Limited_Controlled` and `Controlled` share a common root type which contains two hidden pointers. As a result, any derivation from these two types inherits the hidden components. Types which are not directly derived from `Controlled` or `Limited_Controlled` but contain controlled components utilize a third hidden pointer to act as a root of the component tree. Fig. 2 demonstrates the use of hidden fields.

```
type Ctrl_Deriv is new Controlled with record
   -- Prev inherited from Controlled
   -- Next inherited from Controlled
   . . .
end record;

type Ctrl_Comps is record
   -- _Record_Controller : Finalizable_Ptr;

   Comp1 : Ctrl_Deriv;
   Comp2 : Ctrl_Deriv;
end record;
```

Figure 2: Hidden fields in types

The tree-like representation is constructed during the initialization phase of an object. Fig. 3 presents a simple controlled type with two controlled components along with the actual linkages between all hidden fields.

```
type Ctrl_Comp is new Controlled with record
   -- Prev
   -- Next
   Data : . . .;
end record;

type Ctrl_Typ is new Controlled with record
   -- Prev
   -- Next
   -- _Record_Controller

   Comp1 : Ctrl_Comp;
      -- Prev
      -- Next
      -- Data

   Comp2 : Ctrl_Comp;
      -- Prev
      -- Next ———> null
      -- Data
end record;
```

Figure 3: Linkages at the type level

The compiler generates additional code as part of Initialize and Adjust to respectively create and replicate the tree-like structure of an object. In addition, the GNAT runtime contains support routines which walk the tree and perform adjustment and finalization.

On a more global level, each scope contains a finalization chain, a list header which acts as a collection of objects. All controlled objects which appear in a scope are attached to the corresponding finalization chain. This is where fields Prev and Next of type Ctrl_Typ from Fig. 3 come into play. The compiler adds code to finalize the chain on scope exit. This action simply traverses the collection and finalizes individual objects.

Heap-allocated controlled objects are treated the same way as their stack-allocated counterparts. The only difference is that a finalization chain is now associated with an access-to-controlled type rather than a scope. When an access-to-controlled type goes out of scope, its associated chain is finalized.

3. PERFORMANCE EVALUATION OF THE 95 IMPLEMENTATION

The major benefit of the 95 implementation is its uniformity and maturity. The compiler and runtime generate and use the exact same code to support heap- and stack-allocated objects. On the other hand, the 95 implementation suffers from several drawbacks:

* Size issues - In the best case scenario, a controlled type has two hidden components and in the worst case - three. Object footprint is further increased by multiple controlled components and/or degree of nesting. Consider record type Ctrl_Typ from Fig. 3 - it has 4 source and 7 hidden components.

* Overhead - The complex tree-like representation of a controlled object requires multiple runtime calls to set up and maintain. For instance, it takes 4 calls (Fig. 4) to create the tree for type Ctrl_Typ from Fig. 3. The number of calls increases with the degree of component nesting.

```
Obj : Ctrl_Rec;
-- Attach (Obj.Comp1, To => Obj._Record_Controller);
-- Attach (Obj.Comp2, To => Obj._Record_Controller);
-- Attach (Obj._Record_Controller,
--          To => <chain of objects in scope>);
-- Attach (Obj, To => <chain of objects in scope>);
```

Figure 4: Creation of tree structure for Ctrl_Typ

* Robustness - Data corruption that overlays fields Prev, Next or _Record_Controller may break a chain of components or objects, thereby omitting adjustment or finalization calls. This in turn may create malformed copies or prevent proper resource reclamation and lead to unexpected behaviour.

4. THE 2012 IMPLEMENTATION OF CONTROLLED TYPES

The primary design goal of the 2012 implementation (henceforth referred to as "the new implementation") is to eliminate the issues mentioned in Section 3 and improve overall performance. To achieve this goal, the new implementation is split into two separate mechanisms which support stack-and heap-allocated objects respectively.

4.1 Support for stack-allocated controlled objects

The basic approach of managing stack-allocated controlled objects is inspired by program counter (PC) mapping. A compiler would generate tables which allow for the state of several components or objects to be inferred depending on the value of the PC.

4.1.1 Record types

Instead of mapping addresses, GNAT utilizes a single counter, usually of a numeric type, to represent the state of a component list. Multiple component lists in variant parts require additional counters. Fig. 5 demonstrates the use of a counter to reflect the initialization state of several controlled components.

Note that the state counter is updated to a predetermined value each time a component is successfully initialized.

44

```
procedure Initialize (Obj : in out Ctrl_Rec) is
    C : . . . := 0;
begin
    Initialize (Comp1);
    C := 1;
    Initialize (Comp2);
    C := 2;
end Initialize;
```

Figure 5: Counter use in component initialization

The state counter plays a vital role in partial finalization caused by unsuccessful initialization. Assume that `Initialize (Comp2)` from Fig. 5 raises `Constraint_Error`. The language mandates that any successfully initialized controlled components (`Comp1` in this case) must be finalized in reverse order of declaration. To achieve this, the compiler produces a "jump block" which is very similar to a PC map. The block acts as a switch between the state counter and subsequent finalization calls. Fig. 6 presents the augmented version of the initialization routine.

```
procedure Initialize (Obj : in out Ctrl_Rec) is
    C : . . . := 0;
begin
    Initialize (Comp1);
    C := 1;
    Initialize (Comp2);              -- (1)
    C := 2;
exception                           -- (2)
    when others =>
        case C is                   -- Jump block
            when 2 => goto L2;
            when 1 => goto L1;
            when 0 => goto L0;
        end case;

        <<L2>> Finalize (Comp2);
        <<L1>> Finalize (Comp1);    -- (3)
        <<L0>> raise;               -- (4)
end Initialize;
```

Figure 6: Counter use in partial finalization

When the initialization of `Comp2` fails with `Constraint_Error` (1), control is passed to the exception handler (2). Since the value of counter `C` is 1, the jump block directs the flow of execution to `<L1>` which in turn finalizes `Comp1` (3) and reraises `Constraint_Error` (4).

Finalization of components may itself raise one or more exceptions. The language treats these exceptions as high priority and mandates that only the first such exception be propagated up to the caller. Fig. 7 demonstrates how this exception selection and propagation is achieved.

The initialization routine contains a local variable `Ex` (1) which stores the first exception raised during component finalization. Each call to `Finalize` is encased in a block which stores the current exception only if it is the first one to be raised.

Using the initial setup from Fig. 6, the flow of execution is redirected to `<L1>`, but the finalization of `Comp1` raises `Program_Error` (2). Since this is the first exception encountered during component finalization, it is stored in `Ex` (3).

```
procedure Initialize (Obj : in out Ctrl_Rec) is
    C : . . . := 0;
    Ex : Exception_Occurrence :=        -- (1)
                    No_Exception;
begin
-- Initialization code omitted
exception
    when others =>
        -- Jump block omitted
        -- Finalization of Comp2 omitted

        <<L1>>
        begin
            Finalize (Comp1);           -- (2)
        exception
            when others =>
                if Ex = No_Exception then
                    Save_Occurrence     -- (3)
                        (Current_Exception, To => Ex);
                end if;
        end;
        <<L0>>
        if Ex /= No_Exception then
            raise Ex;                   -- (4)
        end if;
        raise;
end Initialize;
```

Figure 7: Multiple exception recovery mechanism

In the end, Initialize raises `Program_Error` instead of `Constraint_Error` (4).

4.1.2 Array types

The new implementation treats multi-dimensional array types as flat and requires only one state counter per array type. Since the size of each array dimension is always known at initialization time, the compiler does not produce a jump block. Instead, the state counter coupled with the total number of elements in the array is sufficient to infer the state of a multi-dimensional array. Fig. 8 presents the initialization of an array along with partial finalization and exception propagation.

Array initialization starts off by iterating over all dimensions while calling `Initialize` on each individual element (1). Similar to record types, the state counter is updated after each successful initialization (2). If an exception occurs, control is passed to the exception handler (3). At this point, the state counter denotes the number of successfully initialized elements. All those elements must now be finalized in the reverse order of traversal. The counter is updated to reflect the number of uninitialized elements (4). From here on, the reverse iterations skips all uninitialized elements (5) and finalizes those that have been initialized (6). The same exception recovery mechanism used in record types stores the first exception (7) which occurs during finalization and reraises it (8) at the end of the clean up.

4.1.3 Stack-allocated objects

To support initialization and finalization of controlled objects that appear in declarative regions, the new implementation reuses the same approach for record types, but with minor modifications.

The GNAT compiler utilizes a special kind of exception

```
type Ctrl_Array is array (1 .. 10, 2 .. 5) of Ctrl_Rec;

procedure Initialize (Obj : in out Ctrl_Array) is
    procedure Partial_Finalize (C : . . .) is
        Ex : Exception_Occurrence := No_Exception;
    begin
        for Fin_1 in reverse Obj'Range (1) loop
            for Fin_2 in reverse Obj'Range (2) loop
                if C > 0 then
                    C := C - 1;                                        -- (5)
                else
                    begin
                        Finalize (Obj (Fin_1, Fin_2));                 -- (6)
                    exception
                        when others =>
                            if Ex = No_Exception then
                                Save_Occurrence                       -- (7)
                                    (Current_Exception, To => Ex);
                            end if;
                    end;
                end if;
            end loop;
        end loop;
        if Ex /= No_Exception then
            raise Ex;                                                 -- (8)
        end if;
    end Partial_Finalize;

    C : . . . := 0;

begin
    for Dim_1 in Obj'Range (1) loop
        for Dim_2 in Obj'Range (2) loop
            begin
                Initialize (Obj (Dim_1, Dim_2));                      -- (1)
                C := C + 1;                                           -- (2)
            exception                                                 -- (3)
                when others =>
                    C := Obj'Length (1) * Obj'Length (2) - C;         -- (4)
                    Partial_Finalize (C);
                    raise;
            end;
        end loop;
    end loop;
end Initialize;
```

Figure 8: Array initialization

handler called `AT_END` to emulate the Java's "finally" keyword. The handler guarantees that any code within the `AT_END` is executed regardless of the enclosing construct's exception status.

The new implementation relies on the `AT_END` handler to perform finalization actions due to faulty initialization, abnormal statement behaviour or end of scope. Fig. 9 presents a simple scenario of a block containing two controlled objects.

```
declare
    C : . . . := 0;   -- State counter
begin
    Obj1 : Ctrl_Rec;
    Initialize (Obj1);
    C := 1;                -- (1)
    Obj2 : Ctrl_Rec;
    Initialize (Obj2);
    C := 2;                -- (2)
    -- Various source statements
at end
    case C is          -- Jump block
        when 2 => goto L2;
        when 1 => goto L1;
        when 0 => goto L0;
    end case;

    <<L2>> Finalize (Obj2);  -- (3)
    <<L1>> Finalize (Obj1);  -- (4)
    <<L0>>
end;
```

Figure 9: Controlled objects in block

Similar to record components, the state counter `C` is updated once an object is successfully initialized (1). Given normal execution, the value of `C` at the end of the statement list is 2 (2). When the `AT_END` statements are executed, the jump block redirects flow to `<L2>` and both `Obj2` and `Obj1` are finalized (3).

Now assume that `Initialize (Obj2)` raises an exception. The exception prevents proper counter update (2) and passes control to the `AT_END` handler. Since the value of `C` is now 1, the jump block redirects the flow to `<L1>` and only `Obj1` is finalized (4).

4.2 Support for heap-allocated controlled objects

The new implementation manages heap-allocated controlled objects through an entirely different mechanism than the stack-based support outlined in Section 4.1.3. The need for dedicated heap support arises from the fact that controlled types no longer contain hidden fields, therefore they cannot easily form data structures. To address this issue and still maintain low object footprint, the new implementation utilizes a mixed scheme of compiler-generated code and runtime support.

The behaviour of heap-allocated controlled objects is a bit different than that of their stack counterparts. Initialization is carried out in the same semantic manner, but finalization is now associated with the lifetime of the related access type. Fig. 10 explains the dependency between object and type.

When `Inner_Block` goes out of scope (3), the object allocated at (2) must not be finalized because type `Ctrl_Ptr` is still in view. When `Outer_Block` goes out of scope (4), both

```
Outer_Block : declare
    type Ctrl_Ptr is access all Ctrl_Rec;
    Ptr : Ctrl_Ptr := new Ctrl_Rec;      -- (1)
begin
    Inner_Block : declare
        Another_Ptr : Ctrl_Ptr;
    begin
        Another_Ptr := new Ctrl_Rec;  -- (2)
    end Inner_Block;                   -- (3)
    . . .
end Outer_Block;                       -- (4)
```

Figure 10: Lifetime of heap-allocated objects

the objects (1, 2) must be finalized because type `Ctrl_Ptr` is now gone.

To preserve the relation between object and access type, the new implementation introduces an abstraction called a "finalization master". Each finalization master is associated with its related access type and acts as a collection of objects and as a storage pool. Apart from these two roles, a finalization master is also derived from `Limited_Controlled`, with overridden `Initialize` and `Finalize` routines. The master shares the same lifetime as `Ctrl_Ptr` because it is inserted after the type. The master also behaves as a regular stack-allocated controlled object and will be finalized when `Outer_Block` goes out of scope. Together, these two properties ensure the timely finalization of all objects allocated and chained on the master.

4.2.1 Allocation

With a master in place, the implementation can now transform a call to operator **new** into a call to a specialized runtime routine. The routine mimics the profile of `System.Storage_Pools.Allocate`, but utilizes a finalization master instead of a storage pool. The GNAT backend provides the values for object size and alignment. Fig. 11 demonstrates this transformation.

```
-- Original code
-- Ptr : Ctrl_Ptr := new Ctrl_Rec;

Allocate
    (Ctrl_PtrFM,        -- Allocate on the master
     Object_Address,  -- Address of the allocated chunk
     <backend_size>,
     <backend_alignment>);
Ptr := Ctrl_Ptr (Object_Address);
```

Figure 11: Allocation of controlled object

Recall that controlled types no longer contain hidden components, therefore they cannot form data structures. To overcome this issue, `Allocate` must request additional storage space, enough to fit two pointers, and also perform some address arithmetic to hide the two fields. Fig. 12 shows the actual layout of a heap-allocated controlled object.

The two fields `Prev` and `Next` are used to chain a single controlled object onto its related master. The resulting doubly-linked structure allows for the detachment of an object to handle the needs of explicit deallocation. Using Fig. 10 as a reference, the contents of finalization master `Ctrl_TypFM` after `Another_Ptr` is allocated (Fig. 13) are:

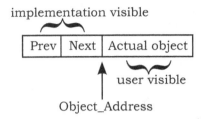

implementation visible

user visible

Object_Address

Figure 12: Layout of a heap-allocated controlled object

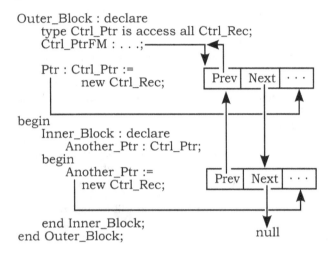

Figure 13: Controlled object chains

4.2.2 Deallocation

The new implementation transforms a call to `Unchecked_Deallocation` into a call to a specialized run-time routine. The routine mimics the profile of `System.Storage_Pools.Deallocate`, but utilizes a finalization master instead of a storage pool. The GNAT backend provides the values for object size and alignment. Deallocate first performs address arithmetic to expose the two hidden fields and then detaches the object from the related finalization master. This action ensures that double finalization will not take place when the master goes out of scope. In the end, the routine reclaims the memory occupied by both the fields and the actual object.

4.2.3 Finalization

The language defines two separate cases where finalization of heap-allocated objects must be carried out.

* Deallocation - The object must be finalized right before it is destroyed. To achieve this, the new implementation inserts a call to `Finalize` right before calling the runtime support routine `Deallocate`.

* Scope exit - The object must be finalized when the related access type goes out of scope.

Once a controlled object has been allocated, it is viewed as a typeless chunk of memory by the heap support mechanism. In its current state, the object cannot be finalized because the implementation cannot establish a connection between raw memory and a concrete type. To overcome this problem, the new implementation utilizes a buffer routine called `Finalize_Address`. The logic behind this procedure is illustrated in Fig. 14.

```
procedure Finalize_Address
          (Obj : System.Address)    -- (1)
is
   type Ptr is access all Ctrl_Rec;  -- (2)
begin
   Finalize (Ptr (Obj).all);        -- (3)
end Finalize_Address;

type Ctrl_Ptr is access all Ctrl_Rec;
Ctrl_PtrFM : Finalization_Master     -- (4)
          (Finalize_Address'Access);
```

Figure 14: Routine Finalize_Address

`Finalize_Address` operates on an address (1) which denotes the start of an object of type `Ctrl_Typ`. The routine creates a local access type (2) which is then used to perform an unchecked conversion of an address to an access value (3). This action restores the type of the object and allows it to be finalized (3). The routine is then associated with the corresponding master (4).

With the help of `Finalize_Address`, a master is now fully capable of finalizing all objects chained onto its list. All the master has to do is iterate over the list and invoke `Finalize_Address` on each memory chunk (object).

5. PERFORMANCE EVALUATION OF THE NEW IMPLEMENTATION

The new implementation is compared to the 95 implementation in four different categories. All tests have been performed on the same machine with respectively 6.4.2 (95 implementation) and 7.0.1 (new implementation) versions of GNAT.

5.1 Object size tests

The following results show the size (in bytes) of the hidden fields pertaining to finalization in a record with N components. Type `Ctrl_Typ` from Fig. 3 would be an example of a record with two controlled components.

.	95 implementation		New implementation	
Comps	Size	Hidden comps	Size	Hidden comps
0	8	2	0	0
1	20	5	0	0
2	28	7	0	0
3	36	9	0	0

The omission of hidden components by the new implementation produces a smaller object footprint.

The following results show the memory consumption (in bytes) of the hidden fields related to finalization in a 10 element array of records with N components. The array is allocated on the heap.

.	95 implementation		New implementation	
Comps	Size	Hidden comps	Size	Hidden comps
0	80	20	8	2
1	160	40	8	2
2	240	60	8	2
3	320	80	8	2

Both implementations rely on hidden pointers to support heap-allocated controlled objects, but the new implementation uses just two for the whole array while the 95 mechanism employs multiple fields per array element.

5.2 Speed and overhead tests

The following results show the time (in seconds) it takes to initialize, adjust and finalize 10,000 records with N components, 50,000 times.

Comps	95 implementation	New implementation
0	8.37	8.77
1	38.30	23.01
2	44.46	27.84
3	53.05	32.07

The state counter approach of the new implementation proves to be less overhead than the tree representation approach of the 95 implementation.

The following results show the time (in seconds) it takes to initialize and finalize 10,000 records with N components, 50 times. This time each 9,990th initialization and each 1,000th finalization raise an exception.

Comps	95 implementation	New implementation
0	6.94	9.86
1	11.90	14.23
2	11.92	14.32
3	11.97	14.72

The complexity and amount of code associated with the exception recovery mechanism of the new implementation account for the poorer performance compared to the 95 implementation. This is a fair trade-off as exception occurrences are rare.

5.3 Code size tests

Due to the amount of code the new implementation produces, the overall size of object files and executables has increased by 4% to 10% compared to the 95 implementation. These numbers have been obtained from customer applications that make heavy use of controlled types. It is worth pointing out that code size grows proportional to the number of controlled types involved whereas data size grows with the number of objects. The same customers reported smaller application footprint at runtime.

5.4 Robustness tests

Robustness is measured in a pass / fail manner because an implementation either successfully performs an action or fails at it. The tests in this category involve overlaying of various controlled objects with junk data to simulate memory corruption and then observing the behavior of adjustment and finalization. It is assumed that code corruption may not occur. In general it is very hard to cause code corruption because programs are generally loaded in protected memory and the code is not allowed to self modify.

95 implementation		New implementation	
Stack	Heap	Stack	Heap
Fail	Fail	Pass	Fail

The 95 implementation fails the robustness tests because memory corruption breaks the tree representation of objects, therefore failing to adjust or finalize various controlled entities. The stack support of the new implementation is not affected by object corruption because the driving engine is code rather than linked structures. The heap support still suffers from broken chains due to overlayed pointers, but this time around the incidence is less frequent as there are only two hidden fields in total per complex object.

6. STATUS AND FUTURE WORK

The new implementation is the default support mechanism for controlled types in the GNAT compiler since early 2012. All efforts are now aimed at reducing the amount of generated code and polishing the implementation.

7. CONCLUSION

This paper explains the 2012 implementation of controlled types in the GNAT compiler. Compared to its predecessor, the new approach is more space efficient, requires less overhead and improves overall robustness. On the other hand, the heap support still suffers when vital components are corrupted and the size of executables grows to reflect the amount of generated code.

8. REFERENCES

[1] C. Comar, G. Dismukes, and F. Gasperoni. The gnat implementation of controlled types. In *Conference Proceedings of TRI-Ada 94*, 1994.

[2] E.Schonberg and B. Banner. The gnat project: A gnu-ada9x compiler. In *Conference Proceedings of TRI-Ada 94*, 1994.

[3] S. T. Taft, R. A. Duff, R. L. Brukardt, E. Ploedereder, and P. L. (Eds.). *Ada 2005 Reference Manual - Language and Standard Libraries*. Springer, Germany, 2006.

HACMS: High Assurance Cyber Military Systems

Kathleen Fisher
DARPA
675 N. Randolph St.
Arlington, VA
kathleen.fisher@darpa.gov

Categories and Subject Descriptors

D.2.4 [**Software Engineering**]: Software/Program Verification; F.3.1 [**Logics and Meanings of Programs**]: Specifying and Verifying and Reasoning about Programs

General Terms

Languages, Security, Reliability

Keywords

High-Assurance Software, Embedded Systems

1. INTRODUCTION

Embedded systems form a ubiquitous, networked, computing substrate that underlies much of modern technological society. Such systems range from large supervisory control and data acquisition (SCADA) systems that manage physical infrastructure to medical devices such as pacemakers and insulin pumps, to computer peripherals such as printers and routers, to communication devices such as cell phones and radios, to vehicles such as airplanes and satellites. Such devices have been networked for a variety of reasons, including the ability to conveniently access diagnostic information, perform software updates, provide innovative features, lower costs, and improve ease of use. Researchers and hackers have shown that these kinds of networked embedded systems are vulnerable to remote attack, and such attacks can cause physical damage while hiding the effects from monitors.

The goal of the HACMS program is to create technology for the construction of high-assurance cyber-physical systems, where high assurance is defined to mean functionally correct and satisfying appropriate safety and security properties. Achieving this goal requires a fundamentally different approach from what the software community has taken to date. Consequently, HACMS will adopt a clean-slate, formal methods-based approach to enable semi-automated code synthesis from executable, formal specifications. In addition to generating code, HACMS seeks a synthesizer capable of producing a machine-checkable proof that the generated code satisfies functional specifications as well as security and safety policies. A key technical challenge is the development of techniques to ensure that such proofs

are composable, allowing the construction of high-assurance systems out of high-assurance components.

Key HACMS technologies include interactive software synthesis systems, verification tools such as theorem provers and model checkers, and specification languages. Recent fundamental advances in the formal methods community, including advances in satisfiability (SAT) and satisfiability modulo theories (SMT) solvers, separation logic, theorem provers, model checkers, domain-specific languages and code synthesis engines suggest that this approach is feasible. If successful, HACMS will produce a set of publicly available tools integrated into a high-assurance software workbench, which will be widely distributed for use in both the commercial and defense software sectors. HACMS intends to use these tools to (1) generate open-source, high-assurance, and operating system and control system components and (2) use these components to construct high-assurance military vehicles. HACMS will likely transition its technology to both the defense and commercial communities. For the defense sector, HACMS will enable high-assurance military systems ranging from unmanned vehicles (e.g., UAVs, UGVs, and UUVs), to weapons systems, satellites, and command and control devices.

2. ACKNOWLEDGMENTS

Distribution Statement A (Approved for Public Release, Distribution Unlimited)

A DSL for Cross-Domain Security

David S. Hardin
dshardin@rockwellcollins.com

Konrad L. Slind
klslind@rockwellcollins.com

Rockwell Collins
Advanced Technology Center

Michael W. Whalen
mike.whalen@gmail.com

Tuan-Hung Pham
hungpt43@gmail.com

University of Minnesota
Software Engineering Center

ABSTRACT

Guardol is a domain-specific language focused on the creation of high-assurance network guards and the specification of guard properties. The Guardol system generates Ada code from Guardol programs and also provides specification and automated verification support. Guard programs and specifications are translated to higher order logic, then deductively transformed to a form suitable for a SMT-style decision procedure for recursive functions over tree-structured data. The result is that difficult properties of Guardol programs can be proved fully automatically.

Categories and Subject Descriptors

F.3.1 [**Specification and Verifying and Reasoning about Programs**]

Keywords

Logics of programs, Mechanical verification, Specification techniques

1. INTRODUCTION

A *guard* is a device that mediates information sharing over a network between security domains according to a specified policy. Typical guard operations include reading field values in a packet, changing fields in a packet, transforming a packet by adding new fields, dropping fields from a packet, constructing audit messages, and removing a packet from a stream.

Guards are becoming prevalent, for example, in coalition forces networks, where selective sharing of data among coalition partners in real time is essential. One such guard, the Rockwell Collins Turnstile high-assurance, cross-domain guard [12], provides directional, bi-directional, and all-way guarding for up to three Ethernet connected networks. See Figure 1 for typical guard usage in a network. The proliferation of guards in critical applications, each with its own specialized language for specifying guarding functions, has

led to the need for a portable, high-assurance guard language.

Figure 1: Typical guard configuration

Guardol is a new, domain-specific programming language aimed at improving the creation, verification, and deployment of network guards. Guardol supports a wide variety of guard platforms, and features the ability to glue together existing or mandated functionality; the generation of both implementations and formal analysis artifacts; and sound, highly automated formal analysis.

Messages to be guarded, such as XML, may have recursive structure; thus a major aspect of Guardol is datatype declaration facilities similar to those available in functional languages such as SML [19] or Haskell [21]. Recursive programs over such datatypes are supported by ML-style pattern-matching. However, Guardol is not simply an adaptation of a functional language to guards. In fact, much of the syntax and semantics of Guardol is similar to that of Ada: Guardol is a sequential imperative language with non-side-effecting expressions, assignment, sequencing, conditional commands, and procedures with **in**/**out** variables. To a first approximation **Guardol = Ada + ML**. This hybrid language supports writing complex programs over complex data structures, while also providing standard programming constructs from Ada.

The Guardol system integrates several distinct components, as illustrated in Figure 2. A Guardol program in file **x.gdl** is parsed and typechecked by the Gryphon verification framework [18] developed by Rockwell Collins. Gryphon provides a collection of passes over Guardol ASTs that help simplify the program. From Gryphon, guard implementations can be generated—at present only in Ada—from Guardol descriptions. For the most part, this is conceptually simple since much of Guardol is a subset of Ada. However,

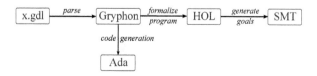

Figure 2: Guardol system components

datatypes and pattern matching need special treatment: the former requires automatic memory management, which we have implemented via a reference-counting style garbage collection scheme; while the latter requires a phase of pattern-match compilation [23]. Since our intent in this paper is mainly to discuss the verification path, we will omit further details.

2. AN EXAMPLE GUARD

In the following we will examine a simple guard written in Guardol. The guard applies a platform-supplied *dirty-word* operation DWO over a binary tree of messages (here identified with strings). When applied to a message, DWO can leave it unchanged, change it, or reject it with an audit string via MsgAudit.

```
type Msg        =  string;
type MsgResult  =  {MsgOK : Msg | MsgAudit : string};
imported function DWO(Text : in Msg, Output : out MsgResult);
```

A MsgTree is a binary tree of messages. A MsgTree element can be a Leaf or a Node; the latter option is represented by a record with three fields. When the guard processes a MsgTree it either returns a new, possibly modified, tree, or returns an audit message.

```
type MsgTree = {Leaf
              | Node : [Value : Msg;
                        Left : MsgTree; Right : MsgTree]};
type TreeResult = {TreeOK : MsgTree | TreeAudit : string};
```

The guard procedure takes its input tree in variable Input; and the return value, which has type TreeResult, is placed in Output. The body uses local variables for holding the results of recursing into the left and right subtrees, as well as for holding the result of calling DWO. The guard code is written as follows:

```
function Guard (Input : in MsgTree, Output : out TreeResult) =
begin
    var ValueResult : MsgResult;
        LeftResult, RightResult : TreeResult;
    in
    match Input with
    MsgTree′Leaf ⇒ Output := TreeResult′TreeOK(MsgTree′Leaf);
    MsgTree′Node node ⇒ begin
        DWO(node.Value, ValueResult);
        match ValueResult with
        MsgResult′MsgAudit A ⇒ Output := TreeResult′TreeAudit(A);
        MsgResult′MsgOK ValueMsg ⇒ begin
            Guard(node.Left, LeftResult);
            match LeftResult with
            TreeResult′TreeAudit A ⇒ Output := LeftResult;
            TreeResult′TreeOK LeftTree ⇒ begin
                Guard(node.Right, RightResult);
                match RightResult with
                TreeResult′TreeAudit A ⇒ Output := RightResult;
                TreeResult′TreeOK RightTree ⇒
                    Output := TreeResult′TreeOK(MsgTree′Node
                              [Value : ValueMsg,
                               Left : LeftTree, Right : RightTree])
```

The guard processes a tree by a pattern-matching style case analysis on the Input variable. There are several cases to consider. If Input is a leaf node, processing succeeds. This is accomplished by tagging the leaf with TreeOK and assigning to Output. Otherwise, if Input is an internal node

(MsgTree′Node node), the guard applies DWO to the message held at the node and recurses through the subtrees (recursive calls are marked with boxes). Complications arise from the fact that an audit may arise from a subcomputation and must be immediately propagated. The code essentially lifts the error monad of the external operation to the error monad of the guard. Note that, throughout, constructors include the name of their datatype; this allows constructor names to be reused.

2.1 Specifying guard properties

Many verification systems allow programs to be annotated with assertions. Under such an approach, a program may become cluttered with assertions and assertions may involve logic constructs. Since we wanted to avoid clutter and shield programmers, as much as possible, from learning the syntax of a logic language, we decided to express specifications using Guardol programs. The key language construct facilitating verification is the *specification* declaration: it presents some code to be executed, sprinkled with assertions (which are just boolean program expressions).

Following is the specification for our example guard. The code runs the guard on the tree t, putting the result in r, which is either a TreeOK element or an audit (TreeAudit). If the former, then the returned tree is named u and the encoded property Guard_Stable, described below, must hold on it. On the other hand, if r is an audit, this means the property is vacuously true.

```
spec Guard_Correct = begin
    var t : MsgTree; r : TreeResult;
    in if ∀(M : Msg). DWO_Idempotent(M) then begin
        Guard(t, r);
        match r with
        TreeResult′TreeOK u ⇒ check Guard_Stable(u);
        TreeResult′TreeAudit A ⇒ skip;
    else skip;
```

The guard code is essentially parameterized by an arbitrary policy (DWO) on how messages are treated. The correctness property simply requires that the result obeys the policy. In other words, suppose the guard is run on tree t, returning tree u. If DWO is run on every message in u, we expect to get u back unchanged, since all dirty words should have been scrubbed out in the passage from t to u. This property is a kind of idempotence, coded up in the function Guard_Stable. The success of the correctness proof depends on the assump-

```
function Guard_Stable (MT : in MsgTree) returns Output : bool =
begin
    var R : MsgResult;
    in
    match MT with
        MsgTree′Leaf ⇒ Output := true;
        MsgTree′Node node ⇒ begin
        DWO(node.Value, R);
        match R with
            MsgResult′MsgOK M ⇒ Output := (node.Value = M);
            MsgResult′MsgAudit A ⇒ Output := false;
        Output := Output and Guard_Stable(node.Left)
                  and Guard_Stable(node.Right);
```

tion that the external dirty-word operation is idempotent on messages, which can be expressed by a computation.

DWO_Idempotent calls DWO twice, and checks that the result of the second call is the same as the result of the

```
function DWO_Idempotent(M : in Msg) returns Output : bool = begin
  var R1, R2 : MsgResult;
  in
  DWO(M, R1);
  match R1 with
    MsgResult'MsgOK M2 ⇒ begin
      DWO(M2, R2);
      match R2 with
        MsgResult'MsgOK M3 ⇒ Output := (M2 = M3);
        MsgResult'MsgAudit A ⇒ Output := false;
    MsgResult'MsgAudit A ⇒ Output := true;
```

first call, taking into account audits. If the first call returns an audit, then there is no second call, so the idempotence property is vacuously true. On the other hand, if the first call succeeds, but the second is an audit, that means that the first call somehow altered the message into one provoking an audit, so idempotence is definitely false.

3. SEMANTIC TRANSLATION

Verification of guards is performed using HOL4 [24] and an SMT solver, such as OpenSMT [4], CVC4 [1], or Z3 [5]. First, a program is mapped into a formal AST in HOL4, where the operational semantics of Guardol have been defined. One can reason directly in HOL4 about programs using the operational semantics; unfortunately, such an approach has limited applicability, requiring expertise in the use of a higher order logic theorem prover. Instead, we would like to make use of the high automation offered by SMT systems. However there is an obstacle: current SMT systems do not understand operational semantics.[1] We surmount the problem in two steps. First, *decompilation into logic* [20] is used to deductively map properties of a program in an operational semantics to analogous properties over a mathematical function equivalent to the original program. This places us in the realm of proving properties of recursive functions operating over recursive datatypes, an undecidable setting in general. The second step is to implement a decision procedure for functional programming [25]. This procedure necessarily has syntactic limitations, but it is able to handle a wide variety of interesting programs and their properties fully automatically.

3.1 Translating programs to HOL

First, any datatypes in the program are defined in HOL (every Guardol type can be defined as a HOL type). Thus, in our example, the types MsgTree, MsgResult, and TreeResult are translated directly to HOL datatypes. Recognizers and selectors, *e.g.*, isMsgTree_Leaf and destMsgTree_Node, for these types are automatically defined and used to translate pattern-matching statements in programs to equivalent if-then-else representations. Programs are then translated into HOL *footprint*[2] function definitions. If a program is recursive, then a recursive function is defined. (Defining recursive functions in higher order logic requires a termination proof; for our example termination is automatically proved.) Note that the HOL footprint function for the guard in Figure 3 is second order due to the external operator DWO: all exter-

nals are held in a record *ext* which is passed as a function argument.

```
Guard ext Input =
 if isMsgTree_Leaf Input then
   TreeResult_TreeOK MsgTree_Leaf
 else let
 ValueResult = ext.DWO((destMsgTree_Node Input).Value)
 in
 if isMsgResult_MsgAudit ValueResult then
   TreeResult_TreeAudit
     (destMsgResult_MsgAudit ValueResult)
 else let
 LeftResult = Guard ext ((destMsgTree_Node Input).Left)
 in
  if isTreeResult_TreeAudit LeftResult then
    LeftResult else let
 RightResult = Guard ext ((destMsgTree_Node Input).Right)
 in
  if isTreeResult_TreeAudit RightResult then
   RightResult
  else
   TreeResult_TreeOK(MsgTree_Node
     [Value := destMsgResult_MsgOK ValueResult;
      Left  := destTreeResult_TreeOK LeftResult;
      Right := destTreeResult_TreeOK RightResult]
```

Figure 3: Footprint function of example guard

Similar translations are made for Guard_Stable and also DWO_Idempotent.

3.2 Guardol operational semantics

The operational semantics of Guardol (see Figure 4) describes program evaluation by an inductively defined judgement saying how statements alter the program state. The formula STEPS Γ *code* s_1 s_2 says "evaluation of statement *code* beginning in state s_1 terminates and results in state s_2". (Thus we are giving a so-called *big-step* semantics.) Note that Γ is an environment binding procedure names to procedure bodies. The semantics follows an approach taken by Norbert Schirmer [22], wherein he constructed a *generic* semantics for a large class of sequential imperative programs, and then showed how to specialize the generic semantics to a particular programming language (a subset of C, for him). Similarly, Guardol is another instantiation of the generic semantics.

Evaluation is phrased in terms of a *mode* of evaluation, which describes a computation state. A computation state is either in Normal mode, or in one of a set of abnormal modes, including Abrupt, Fault, and Stuck. Usually computation is in Normal mode. However, if a Throw is evaluated, then computation proceeds in Abrupt mode. If a Guard command returns false, the computation transitions into a Fault mode. Finally, if the Stuck mode is entered, something is wrong, *e.g.*, a procedure is called but there is no binding for it in Γ.

The rules in Figure 4 are conventional, with the exception of withState which provides a dynamic program-generation facility, used to model blocks and procedure calls.

3.3 Decompilation

The work of Myreen [20] shows how to decompile assembly programs to higher order logic functions; we do the same here for Guardol, a high-level language. A decompilation theorem

---

[1] The main reason for this state of affairs: there is not one operational semantics because each programming language has a different semantics. Another reason: the decision problem for such theories is undecidable.

[2] Terminology lifted from the separation logic literature.

$$[Skip]\frac{}{\text{STEPS } \Gamma \text{ Skip (Normal s) (Normal s)}}$$

$$[Basic]\frac{}{\text{STEPS } \Gamma \text{ (Basic f) (Normal s) (Normal (f s))}}$$

$$[Seq]\frac{\text{STEPS } \Gamma \text{ } c_1 \text{ (Normal } s_1) \text{ } s_2 \qquad \text{STEPS } \Gamma \text{ } c_2 \text{ } s_2 \text{ } s_3}{\text{STEPS } \Gamma \text{ (Seq } c_1 \text{ } c_2) \text{ (Normal } s_1) \text{ } s_3}$$

$$[withState]\frac{\text{STEPS } \Gamma \text{ (f } s_1) \text{ Normal } s_1) \text{ } s_2}{\text{STEPS } \Gamma \text{ (withState f) (Normal } s_1) \text{ } s_2}$$

$$[Cond\text{-}True]\frac{P(s_1) \qquad \text{STEPS } \Gamma \text{ } c_1 \text{ (Normal } s_1) \text{ } s_2}{\text{STEPS } \Gamma \text{ (Cond P } c_1 \text{ } c_2) \text{ (Normal } s_1) \text{ } s_2}$$

$$[Cond\text{-}False]\frac{\neg P(s_1) \qquad \text{STEPS } \Gamma \text{ } c_2 \text{ (Normal } s_1) \text{ } s_2}{\text{STEPS } \Gamma \text{ (Cond P } c_1 \text{ } c_2) \text{ (Normal } s_1) \text{ } s_2}$$

$$[Call]\frac{M.p \in \text{Dom}(\Gamma) \qquad \Gamma(M.p) = c \qquad \text{STEPS } \Gamma \text{ } c \text{ (Normal } s_1) \text{ } s_2}{\text{STEPS } \Gamma \text{ (Call M.p) (Normal } s_1) \text{ } s_2}$$

$$[Call\text{-}NotFound]\frac{M.p \notin \text{Dom}(\Gamma)}{\text{STEPS } \Gamma \text{ (Call M.p) (Normal s) Stuck}}$$

$$[withState]\frac{\text{STEPS } \Gamma \text{ (f } s_1) \text{ Normal } s_1) \text{ } s_2}{\text{STEPS } \Gamma \text{ (withState f) (Normal } s_1) \text{ } s_2}$$

$$[Fault\text{-}Sink]\frac{}{\text{STEPS } \Gamma \text{ c (Fault f) (Fault f)}}$$

$$[Stuck\text{-}Sink]\frac{}{\text{STEPS } \Gamma \text{ c Stuck Stuck}}$$

$$[Abrupt\text{-}Sink]\frac{}{\text{STEPS } \Gamma \text{ c (Abrupt s) (Abrupt s)}}$$

$$[While\text{-}True]\frac{P(s_1) \qquad \text{STEPS } \Gamma \text{ c (Normal } s_1) \text{ } s_2 \qquad \text{STEPS } \Gamma \text{ (While P c) } s_2 \text{ } s_3}{\text{STEPS } \Gamma \text{ (While P c) (Normal } s_1) \text{ } s_3}$$

$$[While\text{-}False]\frac{\neg P(s)}{\text{STEPS } \Gamma \text{ (While P c) (Normal s) (Normal s)}}$$

Figure 4: Evaluation rules

$$\vdash \forall s_1 \text{ } s_2. \text{ } \forall x_1 \ldots x_k.$$
$$s_1.proc.v_1 = x_1 \wedge \cdots \wedge s_1.proc.v_k = x_k \wedge$$
$$\text{STEPS } \Gamma \boxed{code} \text{ (Normal } s_1) \text{ (Normal } s_2)$$
$$\Rightarrow$$
$$\text{let } (o_1, ..., o_n) = \boxed{f(x_1, \ldots, x_k)}$$
$$\text{in } s_2 = s_1 \text{ with}\{proc.w_1 := o_1, \ldots, proc.w_n := o_n\}$$

essentially states that evaluation of *code* implements footprint function f. The antecedent $s_1.proc.v_1 = x_1 \wedge \cdots \wedge s_1.proc.v_k = x_k$ equates $x_1 \ldots x_k$ to the values of program variables $v_1 \ldots v_k$ in state s_1. These values form the input for the function f, which delivers the output values which are used to update s_1 to s_2.[3] Presently, the decompilation theorem only deals with code that starts evaluation in a Normal state and finishes in a Normal state.

3.3.1 The decompilation algorithm

Now we consider how to prove decompilation theorems for Guardol programs. It is important to emphasize that *decompilation is an algorithm*. It always succeeds, provided that all footprint functions coming from the Guardol program have been successfully proved to terminate.

---

[3]In our modelling, a program state is represented by a record containing all variables in the program. The notation $s.proc.v$ denotes the value of program variable v in procedure *proc* in state s. The `with`-notation represents record update.

Before specifications can be translated to goals, the decompilation theorem

$$\vdash \forall s_1 \text{ } s_2. \text{ } \ldots \text{STEPS } \Gamma \boxed{\text{Call}(qid)} \text{ (Normal } s_1) \text{ (Normal } s_2) \Rightarrow \cdots$$

is formally proved for each procedure *qid* in the program, relating execution of the code for procedure *qid* with the footprint function for *qid*.

Decompilation proofs are automated by forward symbolic execution of *code*, using an environment of decompilation theorems to act as summaries for procedure calls. Table 1 presents rules used in the decompilation algorithm. For the most part, the rules are straightforward. We draw attention to the Seq, withState, and Call rules. The Seq (sequential composition) rule conjoins the results of simpler commands and introduces an existential formula ($\exists t. \ldots$). However, this is essentially universal since it occurs on the left of the top-level implication in the goal; thus it can be eliminated easily and occurrences of t can thenceforth be treated as Skolem constants. Both blocks and procedure calls in the Guardol program are encoded using withState. An application of withState stays in the current state, but replaces the current code by new code computed from the current state. Finally, there are two cases with the Call (procedure call) rule:

- The call is not recursive. In this case, the decompilation theorem for *qid* is fetched from the decompilation environment and instantiated, so we can derive

$$\text{let } (o_1, ..., o_n) = f(x_1, \ldots, x_k)$$
$$\text{in } s_2 = s_1 \text{ with } \{qid.w_1 := o_1, \ldots, qid.w_n := o_n\}$$

Table 1: Rewrite rules in the decompilation algorithm

Condition	Rewrite rule
$code = \mathsf{Skip}$	$\vdash \mathsf{STEPS}\ \Gamma\ \mathsf{Skip}\ s_1\ s_2 = (s_1 = s_2)$
$code = \mathsf{Basic}(f)$	$\vdash \mathsf{STEPS}\ \Gamma\ \mathsf{Basic}\ (f)\ (\mathsf{Normal}\ s_1)\ (\mathsf{Normal}\ s_2) = (s_2 = f\ s_1)$
$code = \mathsf{Seq}(c_1, c_2)$	$\vdash \mathsf{STEPS}\ \Gamma\ (\mathsf{Seq}(c_1, c_2))\ (\mathsf{Normal}\ s_1)\ (\mathsf{Normal}\ s_2) =$
	$\quad \exists t. \mathsf{STEPS}\ \Gamma\ c_1\ (\mathsf{Normal}\ s_1)\ (\mathsf{Normal}\ t)\ \wedge \mathsf{STEPS}\ \Gamma\ c_2\ (\mathsf{Normal}\ t)\ (\mathsf{Normal}\ s_2)$
$code = \mathsf{Cond}(P, c_1, c_2)$	$\vdash \mathsf{STEPS}\ \Gamma\ (\mathsf{Cond}(P, c_1, c_2))\ (\mathsf{Normal}\ s_1)\ (\mathsf{Normal}\ s_2) =$
	$\quad \mathsf{if}\ P\ s_1\ \mathsf{then}\ \mathsf{STEPS}\ \Gamma\ c_1\ (\mathsf{Normal}\ s_1)\ (\mathsf{Normal}\ s_2)$
	$\quad\quad\quad\quad \mathsf{else}\ \ \mathsf{STEPS}\ \Gamma\ c_2\ (\mathsf{Normal}\ s_1)\ (\mathsf{Normal}\ s_2)$
$code = \mathsf{withState}\ f$	$\vdash \mathsf{STEPS}\ \Gamma\ (\mathsf{withState}\ f)\ (\mathsf{Normal}\ s_1)\ s_2 = \mathsf{STEPS}\ \Gamma\ (f\ s_1)\ (\mathsf{Normal}\ s_1)\ s_2$
$code = \mathsf{Call}\ qid$	depend on whether the function is recursive or not

where f is the footprint function for procedure qid. We can now propagate the value of the function to derive state s_2.

- The call is recursive. In this case, an inductive hypothesis in the goal—which is a decompilation theorem for a recursive call, by virtue of our having inducted at the outset of the proof—matches the call, and is instantiated. We can again prove the antecedent of the selected inductive hypothesis, and propagate the value of the resulting functional characterization, as in the non-recursive case.

The decompilation algorithm starts by either inducting, when the procedure for which the decompilation theorem is being proved is recursive, or not (otherwise). After applying the rewrite rules, at the end of each program path, we are left with an equality between states. The proof of this equality proceeds essentially by applying rewrite rules for normalizing states (recall that states are represented by records).

3.4 Translating specifications

A Guardol specification is intended to set up a computational context—a state—and then assert that a property holds in that state. In its simplest form, a specification looks like

```
spec name = begin
    var decls
    in
      code;
      check property;
    end
```

where *property* is a boolean expression. A specification declaration is processed as follows. First, suppose that execution of *code* starts normally in s_1 and ends normally in s_2, *i.e.*, assume $\mathsf{STEPS}\ \Gamma\ code\ (\mathsf{Normal}\ s_1)\ (\mathsf{Normal}\ s_2)$. We want to show that *property* holds in state s_2. This could be achieved by reasoning with the induction principle for STEPS, *i.e.*, by using the operational semantics; however, experience has shown that this approach is labor-intensive. We instead opt to formally leverage the decompilation theorem for *code*, which asserts that reasoning about the STEPS-behavior of *code* could just as well be accomplished by reasoning about function f. Thus, formally, we need to show

$$(\mathtt{let}\ (o_1, ..., o_n) = f(x_1, \ldots, x_k)$$
$$\mathtt{in}\ s_2 = s_1\ \mathtt{with}\ \{name.w_1 := o_1, \ldots, name.w_n := o_n\})$$
$$\Rightarrow property\ s_2$$

Now we have a situation where the proof is essentially about how facts about f, principally its recursion equations and induction theorem, imply the property. The original goal has been freed—by sound deductive steps—from the program state and operational semantics. The import of this, as alluded to earlier, is that a wide variety of proof tools become applicable. Interactive systems exemplified by ACL2, PVS, HOL4, and Isabelle/HOL have extensive lemma libraries and reasoning packages tailored for reasoning about recursively defined mathematical functions. SMT systems are also able to reason about such functions, via universal quantification, or by decision procedures, as we discuss in Section 4.

The simple form of specification above is not powerful enough to state many properties. Quite often, a collection of constraints needs to be placed on the input variables, or on external functions. To support this, specification statements allow checks sprinkled at arbitrary points in *code*:

```
spec name =
begin   locals
in
    code[check P_1, ..., check P_n]
end
```

We support this with a program transformation, wherein occurrences of **check** are changed into assignments to a boolean variable. Let $\mathtt{V}$ be a boolean program variable not in *locals*. The above specification is transformed into

```
spec name =
begin
    locals;  V : bool;
in
    V := true;
    code[V := V ∧ P_1, ..., V := V ∧ P_n];
    check(V);
end
```

Thus $\mathtt{V}$ is used to accumulate the results of the checks that occur throughout the code. Every property P_i is checked in the state holding just before the occurrence of $\mathbf{check}(P_i)$, and all the checks must hold. This gives a flexible and concise way to express properties of programs, without embedding assertions in the source code of the program.

Recall the $\mathsf{Guard\_Correct}$ specification. Roughly, it says *If running the guard succeeds, then running* $\mathsf{Guard\_Stable}$ *on the result returns* true. Applying the decompiler to the code of the specification and using the resulting theorem to map from the operational semantics to the functional interpretation, we obtain the goal

$$\left(\begin{array}{l} (\forall m.\ \mathsf{DWO\_Idempotent}\ ext\ m)\ \wedge \\ \mathsf{Guard}\ ext\ t = \mathsf{TreeResult\_TreeOK}\ t' \end{array} \right) \Rightarrow \mathsf{Guard\_Stable}\ ext\ t'$$

which has the form required by our SMT prover, namely that the catamorphism Guard_Stable is applied to the result of calling Guard. However, an SMT prover may still not prove this goal, since the following steps need to be made: (1) inducting on the recursion structure of Guard, (2) expanding (once) the definition of Guard, (3) making higher order functions into first order, and (4) elimination of universal quantification.[4]

To address the first two problems, we induct with the induction theorem for Guard, which is automatically proved by HOL4, and expand the definition of Guard one step in the resulting inductive case. Thus we stop short of using the inductive hypotheses! The SMT solver will do that. The elimination of higher order functions is simple in the case of Guardol since the function arguments (*ext* in this case) are essentially fixed constants whose behavior is constrained by hypotheses. This leaves the elimination of the universals; only the quantification on m in $\forall m$. DWO_Idempotent *ext m* is problematic. We find all arguments of applications of ext.DWO in the body of Guard, and instantiate m to all of them (there's only one in this case), adding all instantiations as hypotheses to the goal.

4. PROVING VERIFICATION CONDITIONS

The formulas generated as verification conditions from the previous section pose a fundamental research challenge: reasoning over the structure and contents of inductive datatypes We have addressed this challenge through the use of a novel decision procedure recently developed by Suter, Dotta, and Kuncak [25]. This decision procedure (we call it SDK) can be integrated into an SMT solver to solve a variety of properties over recursive datatypes. It uses catamorphisms to create abstractions of the contents of tree-structured data that can then be solved using standard SMT techniques. The benefit of this decision procedure over other techniques involving quantifiers is that it is *complete* for a large class of reasoning problems involving datatypes, as described below.

4.1 Catamorphisms

In many reasoning problems involving recursive datatypes, we are interested in *abstracting* the contents of the datatype. To do this, we could define a function that maps the structure of the tree into a value. This kind of function is called a catamorphism [17] or *fold* function, which 'folds up' information about the data structure into a single value. The simplest abstraction that we can perform of a data structure is to map it into a Boolean result that describes whether it is 'valid' in some way. This approach is used in the function Guard_Stable in Section 2. We could of course create different functions to summarize the tree elements. For example, a tree can be abstracted as a number that represents the sum of all nodes, or as a tuple that describes the minimum and maximum elements within the tree. As long as the catamorphism is *sufficiently surjective* [25] and maps into a decidable theory, the procedure is theoretically *complete*. Moreover, we have found it to be *fast* in our initial experiments.

4.2 Overview of the Decision Procedure

The input of the decision procedure is a formula ϕ of literals over elements of tree terms and tree abstractions ($\mathcal{L}_\mathcal{C}$) produced by the catamorphisms. The logic is *parametric* in the sense that we assume a datatype to be reasoned over, a catamorphism used to abstract the datatype, and the existence of a decidable theory C that is the result type of the catamorphism function. The syntax of the parametric logic is depicted in Figure 5.

The syntax of the logic ranges over datatype terms (T and S), terms of a decidable collection theory C. Tree and collection theory formulas F_T and F_C describe equalities and inequalities over terms. The collection theory describes the result of catamorphism applications. E defines terms in the element types contained within the branches of the datatypes. ϕ defines conjunctions of (restricted) formulas in the tree and collection theories. The ϕ terms are the ones solved by the SDK procedure; these can be generalized to arbitrary propositional formulas (ψ) through the use of a DPLL solver [8] which manages the other operators within the formula.

S	::=	$T \mid E$	Constructor args
T	::=	$t \mid \mathbb{C}_j(S_1, \ldots, S_{n_j}) \mid \mathbb{S}_{j,k_\tau}(T)$	Tree terms
C	::=	$c \mid \alpha(T) \mid \mathcal{T}_C$	C-terms
F_T	::=	$T = T \mid T \neq T$	Tree (dis)equations
F_C	::=	$C = C \mid \mathcal{F}_C$	Formula of $\mathcal{L}_\mathcal{C}$
E	::=	variables of type $\mathcal{E}_k \mid \mathbb{S}_{j,k_\mathcal{E}}(T)$	Expression
ϕ	::=	$\bigwedge F_T \wedge \bigwedge F_C$	Conjunctions
ψ	::=	$\phi \mid \neg\phi \mid \phi \vee \phi \mid \phi \wedge \phi \mid$ $\phi \Rightarrow \phi \mid \phi \Leftrightarrow \phi$	Formulas

Figure 5: Syntax of the parametric logic

In the procedure, we have a single datatype τ with m constructors. The j-th constructor ($1 \leq j \leq m$), $\mathbb{C}_j$, has n_j arguments ($n_j \geq 0$), whose types are either τ or $\mathcal{E}$, an element type. For each constructor $\mathbb{C}_j$, we have a list of selectors $\mathbb{S}_{j,k}$ ($1 \leq k \leq n_j$), which extracts the k-th argument of $\mathbb{C}_j$. For type safety, we may put the type of the argument to be extracted as a subscript of its selector. That is, each selector may be presented as either $\mathbb{S}_{j,k_\tau}$ or $\mathbb{S}_{j,k_\mathcal{E}}$. The decision procedure is parameterized by $\mathcal{E}$, a collection type $\mathcal{C}$, and a catamorphism function $\alpha : \tau \rightarrow \mathcal{C}$. For example, the datatype MsgTree has two constructors Leaf and Node. The former has no argument while the latter has three arguments corresponding to its Value, Left, and Right. As a result, we have three selectors for Node, including Value: MsgTree → Msg, Left : MsgTree → MsgTree, and Right : MsgTree → MsgTree. In addition, a tree can be abstracted by the catamorphism Guard_Stable : MsgTree → bool to a boolean value. In the example, $\mathcal{E}$, $\mathcal{C}$, and α are Msg, bool, and Guard_Stable, respectively.

4.3 Implementing Suter-Dotta-Kuncak

The decision procedure works on top of an SMT solver $\mathcal{S}$[5] that supports theories for $\tau, \mathcal{E}, \mathcal{C}$, and uninterpreted functions. Note that the only part of the parametric logic that is not inherently supported by $\mathcal{S}$ is the applications of the catamorphism. Therefore, the main idea of the decision procedure is to approximate the behavior of the catamorphism

---

[4]Some of these steps are incorporated in various SMT systems, *e.g.*, many, but not all, SMT systems heuristically instantiate quantifiers. For a discussion of SMT-style induction see [15].

[5]Suter et al. [26] specifically used Z3 [5] as the underlying SMT solver.

by repeatedly unrolling it a certain number of times and treating the calls to the not-yet-unrolled catamorphism instances at the lowest levels as calls to uninterpreted functions. However, an uninterpreted function can return any values in its co-domain; hence, the presence of these uninterpreted functions can make the sat/unsat result not trustworthy. To address this issue, each time the catamorphism is unrolled, a boolean control condition B is created to determine if the uninterpreted functions at the bottom level are necessary to the determination of satisfiability. That is, if B is true, the list of uninterpreted functions does not play any role in the satisfiability result.

The main steps of the procedure are shown in Algorithm 1. The input of the algorithm is a formula ϕ written in the parametric logic and a program Π, which contains ϕ and the definitions of data type τ and catamorphism α. The goal of the algorithm is to determine the satisfiability of ϕ through repeated unrolling α using the $unrollStep$ function. Given a formula ϕ_i generated from the original ϕ after unrolling the catamorphism i times and the corresponding control condition B_i of ϕ_i, function $unrollStep(\phi_i, \Pi, B_i)$ unrolls the catamorphim one more time and returns a pair (ϕ_{i+1}, B_{i+1}) containing the unrolled version ϕ_{i+1} of ϕ_i and a control condition B_{i+1} for ϕ_{i+1}. Function $decide(\varphi)$ simply calls S to check the satisfiability of φ and returns $SAT/UNSAT$ accordingly.

---

1   $(\phi, B) \leftarrow unrollStep(\phi, \Pi, \emptyset)$
2   **while** *true* **do**
3   **switch** $decide(\phi \wedge \bigwedge_{b \in B} b)$ **do**
4   **case** SAT
5   **return** *"SAT"*
6   **case** $UNSAT$
7   **switch** $decide(\phi)$ **do**
8   **case** $UNSAT$
9   **return** *"UNSAT"*
10   **case** SAT
11                    $(\phi, B) \leftarrow unrollStep(\phi, \Pi, B)$

Algorithm 1: Catamorphism unrolling algorithm [26]

Let us examine how satisfiability and unsatisfiability are determined in the algorithm. In general, the algorithm keeps unrolling the catamorphism until we find a sat/unsat result that we can trust. To do that, we need to consider several cases after each unrolling is carried out. First, at line 4, ϕ is satisfiable and the control condition is true, which means uninterpreted functions are not involved in the satisfiable result. In this case, we have a complete tree model for the SAT result and we can conclude that the problem is satisfiable.

On the other hand, let us consider the case when $decide(\phi \wedge \bigwedge_{b \in B} b) = UNSAT$. The $UNSAT$ may be due to the unsatisfiability of ϕ, or the control condition, or both of them together. As a result, to understand the $UNSAT$ more deeply, we could try to check the satisfiability of ϕ alone, as depicted at line 7. Note that checking ϕ alone also means that the control condition is not used; consequently, the values of uninterpreted functions may contribute to the sat/unsat result of $decide(\phi)$. If $decide(\phi) = UNSAT$ as at line 8, we can conclude that the problem is unsatisfiable because assigning

the uninterpreted functions to any values in their co-domains still cannot make the problem satisfiable as a whole. Finally, we need to consider the case $decide(\phi) = SAT$ as at line 10. Since we already know that $decide(\phi \wedge \bigwedge_{b \in B} b) = UNSAT$, the only way to make $decide(\phi)$ be SAT is by calling to at least one uninterpreted function, which also means that the SAT result is untrustworthy. Therefore, we need to keep unrolling at least one more time as denoted at line 11.

4.4   Tool Architecture

The overall architecture of our solver, called RADA (Reasoning over Abstract Datatypes with Abstraction), is shown in Figure 6. It closely follows the algorithm described in the previous section. We use CVC4 [1] and Z3 [5] as the underlying SMT solvers in RADA because of their powerful abilities to reason about recursive data types. The grammar of RADA in Figure 4.4 is based on the SMT-Lib 2.0 [2] format with some new syntax for selectors, testers, data type declarations, and catamorphism declarations.

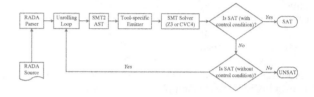

Figure 6: RADA **architecture.**

$\langle datadecl \rangle$	::=	(**declare-datatypes** $\langle datatype \rangle^+$)
$\langle datatype \rangle$	::=	($\langle symbol \rangle$ $\langle datatype\_branch \rangle^+$)
$\langle datatype\_branch \rangle$	::=	($\langle symbol \rangle$ [$\langle branch\_parameter \rangle^+$])
$\langle branch\_parameter \rangle$	::=	($\langle symbol \rangle$ $\langle sort \rangle$)
$\langle catadecl \rangle$	::=	**define-catamorphism** $\langle cata \rangle$)
$\langle cata \rangle$	::=	($\langle symbol \rangle$ ($\langle sort \rangle$) $\langle sort \rangle$ $\langle term \rangle$)
$\langle selector\_application \rangle$	::=	$\langle symbol \rangle$ $\langle symbol \rangle$
$\langle tester\_application \rangle$	::=	is-$\langle symbol \rangle$ $\langle symbol \rangle$]

Figure 7: RADA **grammar.**

Note that although selectors, testers, and data type declarations are not defined in SMT-Lib 2.0, all of them are currently supported by both CVC4 and Z3; therefore, only catamorphism declarations are not understood by these solvers. As a result, to bridge the gap between the input format of RADA and that of CVC4/Z3, each time the catamorphism is unrolled, we build an abstract syntax tree in which the catamorphism declaration is replaced by an uninterpreted function representing the behaviors of the unrolled parts of the catamorphism. Based on the abstract syntax tree, we generate an .smt2 file that CVC4 or Z3 accepts with the help of a tool-specific emitter, which is responsible for creating a suitable .smt2 file for the solver being used.

4.5   Experimental Results

To test our approach, we have developed a handful of small benchmark guard examples. For timings, we focus on the SMT solver which performs the interesting part of the proof search. The results are shown in Table 2, where the last guard is the running example from the paper. In our early experience, the SDK procedure allows a wide variety of interesting properties to be expressed and our initial timing experiments have been very encouraging, despite the relatively naïve implementation of SDK, which we will optimize in the near future. For a point of comparison, we provide a translation of the problems to Microsoft's Z3 in which we use universal quantifiers to describe the catamorphism behavior. This approach is incomplete, so properties that are falsifiable (i.e., return SAT) often do not terminate (we mark this as 'unknown'). A better comparison would be to run our implementation against the Leon tool suite developed at EFPL [26]. Unfortunately, it is not currently possible to do so as the Leon tool suite operates directly over the Scala language rather than at the SMT level. All benchmarks were run on Windows 7 using an Intel Core I3 running at 2.13 GHz.

5. DISCUSSION

As a programming language with built-in verification support, Guardol seems amenable to being embedded in an IVL (Intermediate Verification Language) such as Boogie [16] or Why [7]. However, our basic aims would not be met in such a setting. The operational semantics in Section 3.2 defines Guardol program execution, which is the basis for verification. We want a strong formal connection between a program plus specifications, both expressed using that semantics, and the resulting SMT goals, which do not mention that semantics. The decompilation algorithm achieves this connection via machine-checked proof in higher order logic. This approach is simpler in some ways than an IVL, where there are two translations: one from source language to IVL and one from IVL to SMT goals. To our knowledge, IVL translations are not machine-checked, which is problematic for our applications. Our emphasis on formal models and deductive transformations should help Guardol programs pass the stringent certification requirements imposed on high-assurance guards.

Higher order logic plays a central role in our design. HOL4 implements a foundational semantic setting in which the following are formalized: program ASTs, operational semantics, footprint functions (along with their termination proofs and induction theorems), and decompilation theorems. Decompilation extensively uses higher order features when composing footprint functions corresponding to subprograms. Moreover, the backend verification theories of the SMT system already exist in HOL4. This offers the possibility of doing SMT proof reconstruction [3] in order to obtain even higher levels of assurance. Another consequence is that, should a proof fail or take too long in RADA, it could be performed interactively.

An interesting issue concerns specifications: guard specifications can be about *intensional* aspects of a computation, *e.g.*, its structure or sequencing, as well as its result. For example, one may want to check that data fuzzing operations always occur before encryption. However, our current framework, which translates programs to *extensional* functions, will not be able to use SMT reasoning on intensional properties. Information flow properties [9] are also intensional, since in that setting one is not only concerned with the value of a variable, but also whether particular inputs and code structures were used to produce it. Techniques similar to those in [27] could be used to annotate programs in order to allow SMT backends to reason about intensional guard properties.

5.1 Current and Future Work

We plan to further enhance both language and verification

aspects of Guardol. In recent work, we have built a custom Guardol editor, using the Xtext framework [6]. A screenshot is given in Figure 8. The editor provides conventional support such as keyword highlighting, code completion, and simple semantic processing, such as type-checking. The editor interface also supports the invocation of code generation and verification subsystems.

Figure 8: Xtext-based Guardol editor

The current Guardol language could be made more userfriendly. It is essentially a monomorphic version of ML with second order functions, owing to Guardol's external function declarations. It might be worthwhile to support polymorphic types so that the repeated declarations of instances of polymorphic types, *e.g.*, option types and list types, can be curtailed. Additionally, programs could be considerably more terse if exceptions were in the language, since explicitly threading the error monad wouldn't be needed to describe guard failures.

Planned verification improvements include integration of string solvers and termination deferral. In the translation to SMT, strings are currently treated as an uninterpreted type and string operations as uninterpreted functions. Therefore, the system cannot reason in a complete way about guards where string manipulation is integral to correctness. We plan to integrate a string reasoner, *e.g.*, [13], into our system to handle this problem. The use of string solvers in *web sanitizers* used to defeat cross-site scripting attacks [11] is highly similar to planned applications of Guardol. Moreover, guards and sanitizers have similar requirements, such as idempotence and commutativity.

A weak point in the end-to-end automation of Guardol verification is termination proofs. If the footprint function for a program happens to be recursive, its termination proof may well fail, thus stopping processing. Techniques for defining partial recursive functions have been developed [10, 14]. These approaches allow the derivation of recursion equations and induction theorems constrained by termination requirements. Adopting one of these techniques would remedy this weakness in Guardol, allowing the deferral of termination ar-

Table 2: Experimental results on guard examples

Test #	OpenSMT-SDK	Z3
Guard 1	5 sat (0.83s) / 1 unsat (0.1s)	5 unknown / 1 unsat (0.06 s)
Guard 2	3 unsat (0.28s)	1 unknown / 2 unsat (0.11 s)
Guard 3	3 sat (0.33s) / 4 unsat (0.46s)	1 unknown / 2 sat (0.17s) / 4 unsat (0.42 s)
DWO	1 unsat (0.34s)	1 unsat (0.11s)
MIME	17 unsat (2.0s)	17 unsat (0.2s)

guments while partial correctness proofs are addressed. Of course, termination arguments then need to be automated and we hope to apply RADA to useful subsets of this class of problems.

Arrays are an essential component in any programming language, and Guardol has arrays as a basic type. However, naive approaches to automating proofs of programs that iterate over arrays don't work well. We plan to identify a useful class of iterations over arrays adaptable to the SDK approach. The first obstacle is that general while-loops are not catamorphic. However, we intend to exploit the fact that the class of for loops is primitive recursive, and so every for-loop should have a catamorphic counterpart.

Finally, we plan to verify the correctness of code generated from guards. The general approach will be to relate the footprint function of a guard with the function resulting from decompiling the generated assembly code. Myreen's technology for decompilation of low-level code will be key in this effort.

6. REFERENCES

[1] C. Barrett, C. L. Conway, M. Deters, L. Hadarean, D. Jovanović, T. King, A. Reynolds, and C. Tinelli. CVC4. In *Proceedings of the 23rd international conference on Computer aided verification*, CAV'11, pages 171–177, 2011.

[2] C. Barrett, A. Stump, and C. Tinelli. The SMT-LIB standard: Version 2.0. In A. Gupta and D. Kroening, editors, *Proceedings of the 8th International Workshop on Satisfiability Modulo Theories (Edinburgh, England)*, 2010.

[3] S. Böhme, A. Fox, T. Sewell, and T. Weber. Reconstruction of Z3's bit-vector proofs in HOL4 and Isabelle/HOL. In *Proceedings of Certified Programs and Proofs*, volume 7086 of *LNCS*. Springer, 2011.

[4] R. Bruttomesso, E. Pek, N. Sharygina, and A. Tsitovich. The OpenSMT solver. In *Proceedings of TACAS*, volume 6015 of *LNCS*, 2010.

[5] L. De Moura and N. Bjørner. Z3: An Efficient SMT Solver. In *Proceedings of the Theory and practice of software, 14th international conference on Tools and algorithms for the construction and analysis of systems*, TACAS'08/ETAPS'08, pages 337–340, 2008.

[6] M. Eysholdt and H. Behrens. Xtext: implement your language faster than the quick and dirty way. In *Proceedings of the ACM international conference companion on Object oriented programming systems languages and applications companion*, SPLASH '10, pages 307–309. ACM, 2010.

[7] J.-C. Filliâtre. *Deductive Program Verification*. Thèse d'habilitation, Université Paris 11, Dec. 2011.

[8] H. Ganzinger, G. Hagen, R. Nieuwenhuis, A. Oliveras, and C. Tinelli. DPLL(T): Fast decision procedures. In

Proceedings of CAV, volume 3114 of *LNCS*, pages 175–188. Springer, 2004.

[9] J. Goguen and J. Meseguer. Security policies and security models. In *Proc of IEEE Symposium on Security and Privacy*, pages 11–20. IEEE Computer Society Press, 1982.

[10] D. Greve. Assuming termination. In *Proceedings of ACL2 Workshop*, ACL2 '09, pages 114–122. ACM, 2009.

[11] P. Hooimeijer, B. Livshits, D. Molnar, P. Saxena, and M. Veanes. Fast and precise sanitizer analysis with BEK. In *Proceedings of the 20th USENIX conference on Security*, pages 1–16, Berkeley, CA, USA, 2011. USENIX Association.

[12] R. C. Inc. Turnstile High Assurance Guard Homepage. http://www.rockwellcollins.com/.

[13] A. Kiezun, V. Ganesh, P. Guo, P. Hooimeijer, and M. Ernst. HAMPI: A solver for string constraints. In *Proceedings of ISSTA*, 2009.

[14] A. Krauss. *Automating recursive definitions and termination proofs in higher order logic*. PhD thesis, TU Munich, 2009.

[15] K. R. Leino. Automating induction with an SMT solver. In *Proceedings of VMCAI*, volume 7148 of *LNCS*. Springer, 2012.

[16] K. R. Leino and P. Ruemmer. A polymorphic intermediate verification language: Design and logical encoding. In *Proceedings of TACAS*, volume 6015 of *LNCS*, 2010.

[17] E. Meijer, M. Fokkinga, and R. Paterson. Functional programming with bananas, lenses, envelopes, and barbed wire. In *Proceedings of FPCA*, volume 523 of *LNCS*, 1991.

[18] S. Miller, M. Whalen, and D. Cofer. Software model checking takes off. *CACM*, 53:58–64, February 2010.

[19] R. Milner, M. Tofte, R. Harper, and D. MacQueen. *The Definition of Standard ML (Revised)*. The MIT Press, 1997.

[20] M. Myreen. *Formal verification of machine-code programs*. PhD thesis, University of Cambridge, 2009.

[21] S. Peyton Jones et al. The Haskell 98 language and libraries: The revised report. *Journal of Functional Programming*, 13(1):0–255, Jan 2003.

[22] N. Schirmer. *Verification of sequential imperative programs in Isabelle/HOL*. PhD thesis, TU Munich, 2006.

[23] P. Sestoft. ML pattern match compilation and partial evaluation. In *Dagstuhl Seminar on Partial Evaluation*, volume 1110 of *LNCS*, pages 446–464, 1996.

[24] K. Slind and M. Norrish. A brief overview of HOL4. In

Proceedings of TPHOLs, volume 5170 of *LNCS*, pages 28–32, 2008.

[25] P. Suter, M. Dotta, and V. Kuncak. Decision procedures for algebraic data types with abstractions. In *Proceedings of POPL*, pages 199–210. ACM, 2010.

[26] P. Suter, A. Köksal, and V. Kuncak. Satisfiability modulo recursive programs. In E. Yahav, editor,

Proceedings of Static Analysis, volume 6887 of *LNCS*, pages 298–315. Springer, 2011.

[27] M. Whalen, D. Greve, and L. Wagner. Model checking information flow. In D. Hardin, editor, *Design and Verification of Microprocessor Systems for High-Assurance Applications*. Springer, 2010.

Real-Time Java in Modernization of the Aegis Weapon System

Kelvin Nilsen, Chief Technology Officer Java
Atego Systems
5930 Cornerstone Court West, Suite 250
San Diego, CA 92121
(+1) 801-756-4821
kelvin.nilsen@atego.com

ABSTRACT

The U.S. Navy's Aegis system, considered to be the "shield of the fleet", provides area air defense for a carrier battle group in addition to providing long-range ballistic missile defense. A typical Aegis deployment consists of about 100 computers, many of which have multiple cores. The application is distributed, with typical real-time threads spanning 4 or 5 different computers. End-to-end distributed thread timing constraints measured from stimulus to response are typically under 100 ms. The target jitter constraints on the individual contributions of processors to the end-to-end deadline constraint are well below 1 ms. The system is fully redundant to support fault tolerance. The software is considered to be safety critical because it aims and fires weapons.

The Aegis Weapons System software was recently rewritten into real-time Java as part of the Aegis Modernization activity. This project involved replacement of about 200,000 lines of CMS-2 and Ada code with roughly 500,000 lines of Java. The effort began in 2003 and the new Java implementation of Aegis Weapons System is now being deployed on warships. This paper describes the motivation for the modernization effort and provides a summary of Lockheed Martin's experiences with this project.

Categories and Subject Descriptors

D.3.2 [**Language Classifications**] Concurrent, distributed, and parallel languages, Object-oriented languages, Java; D.2.7 [**Distribution, Maintenance, and Enhancement**]: Corrections, Enhancement, Extensibility, Portability; D.2.11 [**Software Architectures**]: Data abstraction, Information hiding, Languages, Patterns; D.2.13 [**Reusable Software**]: Reusable libraries, Reusable models

General Terms

Design, Reliability, Standardization, Verification

Keywords

Java, Dynamic Storage Management, Real-Time, Safety-Critical, Mission-Critical, High-Integrity Systems, Object Oriented Development, Mixed-Model Deployment

1. INTRODUCTION

The U.S. Navy's Aegis Combat System is known as the shield of the fleet. Aegis uses computers to automatically process data received from powerful radars, allowing Aegis to track threats and automate the launching of missiles to intercept those threats. Aegis provides critical area air defense for battle carrier groups and ballistic missile defense for longer range threats.

The Aegis Combat System is used by the U.S. Navy, the Japan Maritime Self Defense Force, the Spanish Navy, the Royal Norwegian Navy, the Republic of Korea Navy, and most recently, the Royal Australian Navy. Over 100 Aegis warships have been deployed by these six navies. Aegis warships from Spain and the U.S. are now contributing to NATO's European Missile Defense System. The planned Aegis Ashore program will provide land-based deployments of the Aegis Combat System. Current plans are for initial deployments in Romania (2015) and Poland (2018).

Given the critical roles played by the Aegis Combat System software, reliability, availability, and performance are essential requirements. The system must be always vigilant. Recognizing and identifying threats, and automating the responses to perceived threats must be performed consistently within very tight timing constraints. The computations required to automate the responses are complex. Since the exact nature of enemy threats cannot be fully anticipated in advance, the software must be very dynamic and adaptive.

A typical Aegis Combat System deployment consists of approximately 100 computers, many of which are multi-core. The computers are configured to provide fully redundant data and processing capabilities. Many operations performed by the Aegis system have end-to-end deadline constraints of 100 ms or less. The typical time-constrained operation involves contributions from many different computers. The jitter constraints on the tasks performed by individual computers are well below 1 ms. The system is considered to be safety critical because it is responsible for aiming and firing weapons.

The Challenge. The original Aegis Combat System ran on proprietary UYK computers designed by the military, running proprietary software written in a combination of the Ada 95 and proprietary CMS-2 programming languages. The original architecture is illustrated in Figure 1. The Navy found that the heavy dependency on proprietary technologies resulted in excessive costs and ineffective operations. As the system began to age, Navy war fighters found they were using computer technologies that were decades older than the most currently available commercial processors. Due to the effects of Moore's law, Navy Aegis computers were hundreds of times slower than the popular gaming computers of the day.

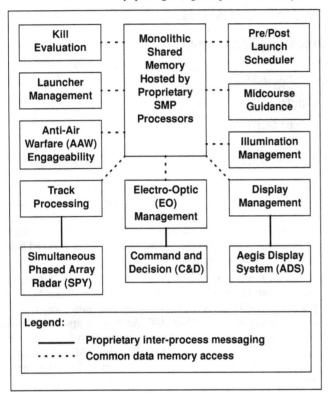

Figure 1. Original (Legacy) Aegis Architecture

The Navy began the shift to COTS (commercial off-the-shelf) hardware components in the 1990s. This leveraged commercial economies of scale, providing much more powerful computers for much lower costs than the previous generation of proprietary hardware. But the Navy found that its software architecture still represented an impediment to timely deployment of state-of-the-art COTS hardware. With each new COTS hardware configuration, significant calendar time and engineering costs were required to port and integrate the Aegis Combat Systems software onto the new platform. With Aegis baseline 7, for example, hardware was selected in 1998, but the upgraded implementation could not be deployed until 2005. As the first of many ships was upgraded, the computers were already 7 years behind the current state of the art.

In 2003, Lockheed Martin, under contract to the U.S. Navy undertook to modernize the Aegis software architecture. There were two primary objectives:

1. To decouple hardware from software, enabling all deployed Aegis Combat Systems to undergo hardware upgrades every 4 years and software upgrades every 2 years, on a staggered schedule.

2. To enable competitive bidding for new software capabilities, with new software components easily integrated into the existing software infrastructure without compromising existing software capabilities.

This initiative was to be known as Aegis Open Architecture.

2. THE SOLUTION

Lockheed Martin reviewed various options for the Aegis Open Architecture. In their experiments, they found that HotSpot Java code ran comparable to C++ on an experimental 250 ms periodic workload. At the same time, they found that the Java language provided superior abstraction and encapsulation than C++, and they judged that retraining their existing staff of CMS-2 and Ada programmers to become effective in Java would have lower risks than attempting to train them in C++.

Given the need for predictable and reliable compliance with sub-ms timing constraints, Lockheed Martin evaluated a number of alternative approaches to real-time Java. Ultimately, they chose to use Atego's Aonix Perc Ultra virtual machine [4] (hereafter referred to as simply PVM), both in single-core and multi-core configurations.

PVM is the most widely deployed and most mature real-time virtual machine in the market. Unlike most of its competitors, it does not implement the Real-Time Specification for Java (RTSJ) [5]. Atego has carefully weighed the benefits and costs associated with supporting the RTSJ specification. So far, its analysis has concluded that the costs far outweigh the benefits. Specific concerns include the following:

1. As a real-time solution for Java, PVM has a much longer history and a more proven track record. PVM has been commercially available since 1997. It has been successfully deployed in hundreds of thousands of devices, with many millions of hours of demonstrated availability at five-nines and higher. It is difficult to find success stories based on RTSJ, and the few vendors who once claimed RTSJ compliance for it now seem to be retreating from this technology.

2. PVM is based on standard edition Java with special implementation techniques to enable reliable and portable real-time operation. In contrast, RTSJ approaches to real-time Java require developers to use the specialized APIs of the RTSJ to achieve real-time behavior. These specialized RTSJ APIs are less desirable because:

   a. Off-the-shelf Java functionality is not compatible with the RTSJ APIs and must be rewritten in order to achieve real-time behavior.

   b. The RTSJ APIs are very difficult to use and their use is error prone.

   c. The RTSJ APIs do not offer the portability, maintainability, and scalability benefits of traditional Java.

   d. The RTSJ APIs add considerable complexity to application code and to virtual machine implementation, making it much more difficult to satisfy safety and security audits.

   e. The RTSJ incurs speed and space overheads that are unacceptable in many real-time systems.

3. In situations that require lower level capabilities than are suitable for standard edition Java (such as compliance with hard real-time constraints, implementation of device drivers and interrupt handlers, and DO-178C level A safety certification), technologies based on JSR-302 such as the Aonix Perc Pico product are much better suited than vanilla RTSJ.

While PVM supports standard edition Java, it also provides a variety of enhanced capabilities to uniquely qualify its use in mission-critical real-time applications development. Several of these capabilities are described below.

The VM Management API. A Java virtual machine is a sophisticated run-time environment, providing many more high-level services than typical minimalist real-time operating systems. In order to provide the full generality required by real-time developers, PVM has even more internal sophistication than other embedded virtual machines. Achieving optimal system performance depends on finding appropriate balances between the memory and CPU-time budgets assigned to application threads and to certain background maintenance activities. By providing APIs to access and control this information, PVM makes it possible for software agents to take responsibility for self configuration of the embedded system. Compare this to the mini- and mainframe computer markets of previous decades, in which full-time staffs were often required to continually monitor and adjust performance parameters, and some companies made entire business out of providing software tools that assist with this effort.

Understanding what is happening inside the virtual machine, and configuring the virtual machine for optimal performance with a given workload, requires visibility into the internal operation of the virtual machine and requires that software be able to adjust the virtual machine configuration on the fly. PVM's management APIs make this possible. Some of the provided services include:

- Query and modify the maximum number of heap allocation regions.
- Query and modify the rate for expansion of the memory allocation heap.
- Query and modify the frequency and priority at which increments of garbage collection work are performed.
- Determine how much CPU time has been dedicated to execution of particular Java threads.
- Determine which synchronization monitors are locked by particular threads, and which threads are waiting for access to particular synchronization monitors (to enable analysis of deadlock and resource contention bottlenecks).
- Obtain a snapshot of the stack back trace for a particular thread, to see what code it is executing at any particular moment.
- Determine the number of I/O requests issued by a particular thread.
- Query and control whether eager linking is enabled.
- Query and control whether JIT compilation is enabled.
- Query and control whether byte-code verification is enabled.
- Query the RTOS priority at which PVM threads run. (Override the default value when you start up the PVM virtual machine.)
- Query the duration of a PVM thread's tick period and time-slice duration. (Override the default values when you start up the PVM.)
- Determine how much time the PVM has been idle, and how much CPU time has been consumed at each priority level (to assist with rate-monotonic scheduling analysis).

The Perc Shell. The Perc shell provides a command-line interface to allow human operators to interactively query and control virtual machine behavior. The shell runs in a dumb terminal connected to a serial port or in a telnet window connected by ethernet. Each PVM supports multiple shells running concurrently.

The Perc shell provides access to all of the VM management services described above. Developers can use the shell to list threads and monitors, view lists of open files and sockets, and examine the "lost file list", which identifies files and sockets that were reclaimed by the garbage collector before they had been closed by the application. Additionally, the shell supports various user conveniences including file system directories, redirection of standard input and output, and wildcard file naming. Users can extend the shell by writing new Java classes.

Dynamic Memory Management. One of the high-level productivity aids provided by the Java programming language is garbage collection, a service which automatically reclaims and recycles memory that had been previously allocated to serve a temporary need and is no longer being used by the application.

All commercially available Java virtual machines collect garbage, but some implementations do it better than others. Conservative and partially conservative garbage collectors make conservative estimates of which memory is still being used. This means they cannot guarantee to reclaim all of the dead memory in the system and usually cannot defragment memory by relocating in-use objects to consecutive memory locations. Note that a single dead object that is improperly identified as live may hold references to an arbitrarily large collection of additional dead objects, all of which must be conservatively treated as live. Thus, the memory for these dead objects cannot be reclaimed.

A key point in understanding conservative garbage collection is that the garbage collector is not always able to distinguish between memory locations that contain pointers and those that contain scalar data such as integer or floating point values. When the garbage collector examines these questionable words of memory, it asks itself the question: "If this in-memory value is a pointer, which object would it refer to?" It then treats the referenced object, if there is one, as live. Note that no amount of testing will guarantee that conservative garbage collection will reliably reclaim the dead memory associated with your application. A memory cell that holds a date and time, for example, might consistently be recognized as a non-pointer during testing. However, when the deployed software is exposed to the full range of possible date and time values, it is likely that certain combinations of values will be perceived by the conservative garbage collection system as references to Java objects, and this will cause unwanted retention of unpredictable amounts of dead memory.

Unlike the garbage collection systems used by other Java virtual machines, PVM uses unique patent-protected real-time garbage collection that is accurate, incremental, defragmenting, and paced. This means that (1) there are no risks of running out of memory because of conservative approximations made by less sophisticated garbage collection systems, (2) both performance and reliability of memory allocation benefit from the PVM garbage collector's ability to defragment memory, and (3) a properly configured PVM will not experience unpredictable stalls at arbitrary times because of interference from the garbage collector.

Real-Time Garbage Collection. Because automatic garbage collection reads and writes the same in-memory objects that Java application threads manipulate, it is necessary to carefully coordinate these independent activities. Because of this coordination requirement, it is common for Java threads running on other virtual machines to experience periods of time when they cannot run because the garbage collector is performing certain critical operations that cannot be interrupted. The duration of these garbage collection interruptions depends on the virtual machine architecture and its configuration. Often, the bound on garbage collection delays is proportional to the size of the allocation heap. Users of alternative virtual machines have reported garbage collection delays ranging from 1 second to tens of seconds with real-world applications. Though these interruptions may be rare, the costs of experiencing a long garbage collection delay at an inopportune time may include mild end-user irritation, lost customers, failed transactions, dropped telephone calls, or manufacturing defects. For example, one large electronic banking organization reported that it had experienced tens of seconds of garbage collection delays with an enterprise-class virtual machine just before market trading ended, forcing the bank to sit on millions of dollars worth of transactions over a weekend.

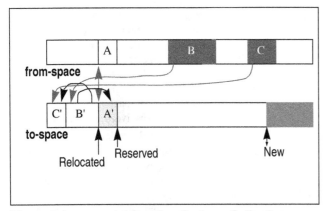

Figure 2. Incremental Copying Garbage Collection

One of the first innovations introduced in the PVM is its patent-protected real-time garbage collection system. The PVM garbage collector divides its effort into thousands of small uninterruptible increments of work. Depending on the choice of underlying CPU, the maximum time required to execute an increment of garbage collection is less than 100 μs. When garbage collection resumes following preemption by a higher priority application thread, it resumes where it left off. There is never a need to go back and restart any phase of garbage collection.

Figure 2 illustrates the incremental copying garbage collection technique used within the PVM. At the start of garbage collection, *from-space* contains the three live objects A, B, and C and *to-space* is empty. Garbage collection consists of incrementally reserving space and subsequently relocating each of the live objects. Any attempt to access the object during garbage collection is automatically redirected to the single valid copy of the object. At the time this snapshot was drawn, the valid versions of objects B and C are B' and C' respectively. The valid version of A is A itself, because this object has not yet been relocated. Each of the invalid versions maintains a pointer to the valid version, colored blue in the illustra-

tion. Objects waiting to be relocated, such as A, also maintain a forwarding pointer to the memory that has been reserved to hold the eventual copy. As objects are being relocated, each pointer contained within the object is replaced by a pointer to the new *to-space* copy of the referenced object. Thus, object B' holds pointers to A' and C', whereas object B held pointers to A and C. A beneficial side effect of copying garbage collection is that the unused memory scattered throughout *from-space* is coalesced into a single larger free segment, from which new memory requests that are issued while garbage collection is taking place can be served.

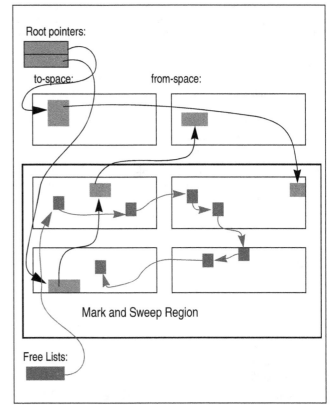

Figure 3. Mostly Stationary Real-Time Garbage Collection

The PVM divides the memory allocation pool into multiple equal-sized regions. On each pass of the garbage collector, two regions are selected as *to-* and *from-space* respectively. These regions are defragmented using the incremental copying garbage collection technique. The unused memory in the other regions is reclaimed using an incremental mark and sweep technique which does not relocate objects. In typical situations, the mark-and-sweep technique achieves the highest memory utilization, but runs the risk of arbitrarily poor utilization in the rare event that it experiences severe memory fragmentation. Incremental copying garbage collection achieves guaranteed utilization of approximately 50%. Depending on workload characteristics and risk-reward profiles, users of the PVM can configure the memory allocation pool for a small number of very large regions (with guaranteed defragmentation, but lower expected memory utilization) or a large number of relatively smaller regions (with better typical memory utilization, but higher risk of fragmentation degradation).

An important unique attribute of the PVM garbage collector is that the total effort required to complete garbage collection is bounded by a configuration-dependent constant, regardless of how much memory has recently been allocated or discarded, and independent of how many times the garbage collector is preempted by application threads. Given this property, it is straightforward to schedule garbage collection to periodically reclaim all of the dead memory in the system. The VM Management API allows garbage collection scheduling parameters to be adjusted on the fly in order to accommodate changes in the system workload. We call this *garbage collection pacing*. This makes sure that the system never exhausts its allocation free pool. If a virtual machine does not support pacing of garbage collection, then it is possible to experience situations in which a low-priority task allocates memory subsequently desired by a high priority task, thereby forcing the high priority task to wait for garbage collection to complete before it can advance. This is an example of priority inversion that is nearly impossible to avoid with most implementations of the Java virtual machine, but is easily avoided with the PVM.

The objective of garbage collection pacing is to make sure that garbage collection gets enough increments of CPU time to make sure it consistently replenishes the allocation pool before the available supply of memory has been exhausted. Figure 4 shows a simulated

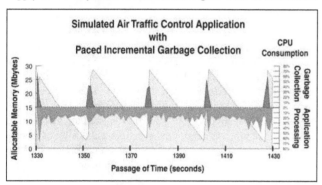

Figure 4. Allocatable Memory vs. Time

air traffic control workload with real-time garbage collection running under the direction of a real-time pacing agent. This particular application is running in a fairly predictable steady state as characterized by the following observations. First, the slope of the yellow chart, which represents the amount of memory available for allocation, is roughly constant whenever garbage collection is idle. This means the application's allocation rate is approximately constant. Second, the heights of the yellow chart's peaks are roughly identical. This means the amount of live memory retained by the application is roughly constant. In other words, the application is allocating new objects at approximately the same rate it is discarding old objects. Finally, the percentage of CPU time required for application processing is well behaved, ranging from about 20% to 50%.

Note that garbage collection is idle most of the time. As memory becomes more scarce, garbage collection begins to run. When garbage collection runs, it interferes with some, but not all, of the real-time application processing. For this reason, you'll note a slight dip in application processing each time the garbage collector, represented by the occasional red upward spikes, runs. You'll also

note a tendency for application processing to briefly increase following each burst of garbage collection. This is because the preempted application needs to perform a small amount of extra work to catch up with real-time scheduling constraints following each preemption.

When properly configured, the pacing agent will carefully avoid delaying the application threads by any more than the allowed scheduling jitter. Configuration parameters to the pacing agent allow specification of the priorities at which garbage collection runs, safety buffers to accommodate transient bursts of high workload activity, and a maximum CPU utilization budget for garbage collection activities. This allows the garbage collection activities to be treated the same as application tasks in the rate monotonic analysis of schedulability.

Priority Inheritance. Because Java was designed to support multiple threads, the language has built-in support for synchronization locks. A synchronization lock allows an individual thread to lock out other threads from performing certain operations while the first thread manipulates shared data. To avoid *priority inversion*, in which a medium priority thread indirectly prevents a high priority thread from making forward progress, the PVM supports a protocol known as *priority inheritance*. When the high-priority task blocks because it needs access to a lock held by a lower-priority thread, the low-priority thread inherits the high priority of the requesting thread. This allows the low priority thread to temporarily elevate its priority in order to preempt any intermediate-priority threads so that the low-priority thread can finish its work and get out of the way of the high-priority thread that desires access to the shared lock.

Precise Timers. Another example of a way in which the PVM has been customized to better support the needs of real-time programmers is our real-time implementation of the standard java.util.Timer class. This class provides an ability to schedule periodic execution of certain Java tasks. The problem with the traditional implementation of these services is that if someone adjusts the real-time clock of the underlying operating system, the periodic behavior of tasks is compromised. Prompted by a key telecommunications customer, Aonix developed an alternative to java.util.Timer in order to provide consistent periodic execution of timer tasks, even if the system clock is modified during execution.

Symmetric Multi-Processor (SMP) Support. The PVM has recently been enhanced to support real-time operation also on multiprocessor systems. The SMP version of PVM fully exploits all of the processors available on an underlying SMP architecture as long as your application has been structured so that sufficient numbers of Java threads are always ready to run. The garbage collection algorithms have been enhanced so that the total effort of garbage collection can be divided between multiple processors. Thus, the wall-clock time required to complete garbage collection on a 4-processor platform is approximately one fourth the time required to collect the same total amount of garbage on a single processor. Pacing of garbage collection in the SMP environment uses the same techniques that are used in the uniprocessor version of PVM.

3. THE RESULTS

Lockheed Martin considers the Aegis Open Architecture project a

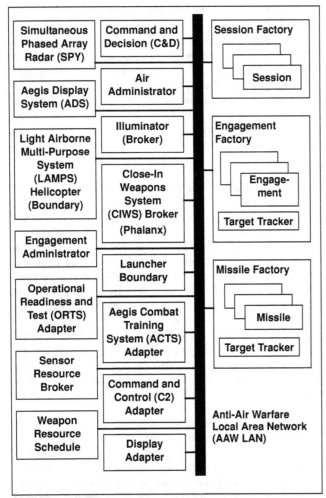

Figure 5. Modernized Aegis Open Architecture Computing Environment (OACE)

tremendous success, reporting significant cost and calendar time savings along several dimensions. The modernized architecture is illustrated in Figure 5. Reported benefits include the following.

1. The existing staff of software engineers, most of whom were previously proficient mainly in CMS-2 and Ada, adapted very quickly to Java.

2. The Eclipse integrated development environment, debugging capabilities, and other off-the-shelf Java development tools represented huge improvements over the capabilities that had been available previously with their proprietary technologies.

3. The newly trained Aegis software engineers implemented the Aegis Air Defense Warfare software, consisting of 150,000 significant lines of code, in only 18 months, including test and evaluation and full requirements verification.

4. Lockheed Martin verified 3,500 requirements to the satisfaction of their Navy customer in only 5 months. This represented a nine-fold improvement over previous experience. Lockheed

Martin attributes this huge productivity gain to the portability benefits of Java. For non-performance related requirements, they were able to run their tests on faster, larger memory Windows computers. Approximately 80% of the verification testing was performed in a Windows environment with a test framework.

5. The first deployment based on the new Aegis Open Architecture required only three years from hardware selection to on-ship hardware refresh, compared to seven years or longer previously.

6. PVM's unique ability to deploy Java programs as native-translated binary programs made it easier to satisfy U.S. Navy security export requirements. The U.S. Navy does not distribute source code to foreign allies and Java byte code is considered too easy to reverse engineer.

7. After completing the Aegis Open Architecture refresh, support was added for the new "Standard Missile 6" with only 3 additional months of development effort. Based on experiences with the legacy Aegis implementation, they would have expected a minimum of a full year of additional development to add support for a new missile.

4. CONCLUSIONS

While different technologies offer different technical strengths and weaknesses, selecting between alternative technologies for the foundation of a large defense application involves much more than a comparison of respective technical merits. Economic factors are also critically important. These can be affected by the popularity of particular technologies, the number of vendors and not-for-profit organizations that are supporting the technologies, the availability of reusable software components and off-the-shelf tools that can be applied to the project's objectives, the sizes and quality of recruiting pools for obtaining engineers to work on the project, and the ease with which existing engineers can be retrained to become proficient in the use of the new technologies.

For modernization of the Aegis Weapons Control Software, Lockheed Martin chose to use a real-time version of Standard Edition Java. Both the initial development effort and several subsequent maintenance activities have benefitted greatly from this choice. Lockheed Martin reports a nine-fold improvement in certain requirements verification activities, a four-fold improvement in the time required to integrate new missile capabilities, and more than a two-fold improvement in the time required to integrate new capabilities into deployed warships.

5. BIBLIOGRAPHY

[1] K. Arnold, J. Gosling, D. Holmes. *The Java™ Programming Language, 4th edition*. 928 pages. Prentice Hall PTR. Aug., 2005.

[2] R. Stanton, *Transitioning Legacy Proprietary Systems to Open Architecture*, Marine Systems and Technology 2010, Rome, Italy

[3] A. Winkler, *The Modernization of the Aegis Fleet with Open Architecture*, Keynote address presented at Java Technology for Real-Time and Embedded Systems, Sept. 2011, York, UK.

[4] K. Nilsen, *Differentiating Features of the PERC Virtual Machine*, http://www.atego.com/downloads/support/white-papers/Differentiating_Features_of_the_Perc_VM.pdf

[5] G. Bollella, B. Brosgol, J. Gosling, P. Dibble, S. Furr, M. Turnbull, *The Real-Time Specification for Java*, Addison Wesley Longman, 195 pages, Jan. 15, 2000.

[6] K. Nilsen, *Making Effective Use of the Real-Time Specification for Java*, Atego White Paper, September 2004, available at http://research.atego.com/jsc/rtsj.issues.9-04.pdf.

[7] D. Locke, B. S. Andersen, B. Brosgol, M. Fulton, T. Henties, J. Hunt, J. Nielsen, K. Nilsen, M. Schoeberl, J. Tokar, J. Vitek, A. Wellings. *Safety-Critical Java Technology Specification, Public Draft*, version 0.78, Oct. 2010, available at http://www.jcp.org/en/jsr/detail?id=302.

[8] M. Richard-Foy, T. Schoofs, E. Jenn, L. Gauthier, K. Nilsen. "Use of PERC Pico for Safety Critical Java", *Conference Proceedings: Embedded Real-Time Software and Systems*, Toulouse, France, May 2010.

[9] J. Durbin, R. Scharading. "The Modernization of the Aegis Fleet with Open Architecture", *Conference Proceedings System and Software Technology Conference*, Salt Lake City, UT, May 2011.

[10] K. Nilsen. "Improving Abstraction, Encapsulation, and Performance within Mixed-Mode Real-Time Java Applications." *Conference Proceedings of the ACM JTRES '07 5th International Workshop on Java Technologies for Real-Time and Embedded Systems*, Vienna, Austria, September, 2007.

FAA's Controller Pilot Automatic Data Communication (Data Comm) System Software Development

Jeffrey O'Leary
En Route and Oceanic Services Directorate
Federal Aviation Administration (FAA)
Washington, DC
jeff.oleary@faa.gov

Alok Srivastava
TASC, Inc.
Washington, DC
asrivastava@yahoo.com

ABSTRACT

To meet future demands and avoid gridlock in the sky and at airports, US Federal Aviation Administration's (FAA) NextGen Data Communications (DataComm) Program is designed to advance today's analog voice-only air-to-ground communications system to one in which digital communications become an alternate and eventually predominant mode of communication.

Categories and Subject Descriptors

D.2.9 [**Software Engineering**]: Management – *lifecycle, software configuration management, software quality assurance (SQA).*

Keywords

NextGen, DataComm, digital communication

1. INTRODUCTION

To meet future demands and avoid gridlock in the sky and at airports, US Federal Aviation Administration's (FAA) NextGen Data Communications (DataComm) Program is designed to advance today's analog voice-only air-to-ground communications system to one in which digital communications become an alternate and eventually predominant mode of communication. Therefore, DataComm is a key transformational program within the FAA's NextGen efforts and a critical next-step in improving air safety, reducing delays, increasing fuel savings, and reducing emissions.

Because of DataComm's projected reduction in voice communications congestion and related errors, the FAA estimates that digital data communications will enable controllers to safely handle approximately 30 percent more traffic than with current systems. In the evolution to NextGen, data communications will advance air traffic control from minute-by-minute instructions to collaborative management of flights from takeoff to landing.

Data communications is an extraordinarily complex integration challenge. On the FAA side, implementation of data communications requires coord/sync/integration of data across several major FAA automation systems, as well as integration of multiple networks spanning separate security domains, and will require a robust Very High Frequency (VHF) air-to-ground communications link.

The data communications network on the ground will interface with Air Traffic Control (ATC) automation platforms - the Tower Data Link Services system for airport towers, and the En Route Automation Modernization (ERAM) system being installed at 20 nationwide En Route centers (ARTCCs). On the aircraft side, data communications will affect the radio, communications management unit, and, in most cases, the aircraft's flight management system.

The current implementation dates, targeted by the DataComm Program, are late 2014 for departure clearances and revisions, and 2016 for En-Route services. Significant work is underway to provide the necessary software enhancements to domain automation software. The ERAM contract with Lockheed Martin is being used to provide a National Logon Capability and a Protocol Gateway, required for both Tower and En Route services. The main "programmatic" challenge in the evolution of DataComm is getting ERAM application software modified, Tower Data Link Services (TDLS) automation platforms developed, and integrating the end-to-end system. The fundamental technical /integration challenge is integrating data communications into air-traffic management procedures. This will, in effect, change the way the controller and pilots perform their jobs, enabling considerable efficiency gains for airspace users.

This presentation will detail software development, challenges in the integration, and lessons learned to date during the implementation of DataComm. Significant portions of the system are under development using Ada, and involve making changes in the biggest modern Ada-based system, ERAM. DataComm will compel changes in onboard software which is also mostly in Ada. Unique challenges have been encountered in meeting the security/integrity requirements while transmitting data between the ATC centers and the aircraft. The presentation will also include a brief discussion on assurance issues and problems, and how Ada and the processes have been adapted as well as mitigations that reduce the dependence on assurance and redevelopment of the commercial products. The initial set of DataComm services will include revised departure clearances, weather reroutes, tailored arrival flight paths, direct-to-fix, and crossing restrictions.

The FAA's DataComm program office plans to conduct trials at designated towers in 2013, and to launch formal integration testing in October of that year. Formal Operational Test and Evaluations (OT&E) of the system is linked to ERAM's full field operational function. After successful completion of OT&E, the DataComm Program will begin deploying services to 73 Towers in 2015.

Synchronization Cannot be Implemented as a Library

Geert Bosch

AdaCore

104 Fifth Avenue

New York, NY 10011, USA

bosch@adacore.com

ABSTRACT

Writing efficient programs for increasingly parallel computer architectures requires the use of hardware primitives, such as atomic read-modify-write instructions or transactional memory. While new libraries and language constructs are introduced to expose the new capabilities, we argue that they are implementation details best left hidden. High-level synchronization constructs, such as those provided by Java and Ada, are both sufficient and necessary for modern programming languages to take full advantage of today's and tomorrow's hardware. While defined in terms of mutual exclusion, we show that these constructs are general enough to allow an enhanced compiler to automatically generate the appropriate lock-free synchronization code for the target system. Language support for synchronization is necessary for efficient, reliable and portable programs.

Categories and Subject Descriptors

D.1.3 [**Programming Techniques**]: Concurrent Programming; D.3.3 [**Programming Languages**]: Language Constructs and Features—*concurrent programming structures*; D.3.4 [**Programming Languages**]: Processors—*compilers, optimization*

Keywords

lock-free synchronization, transactional memory, compiler optimization

1. INTRODUCTION

Writing correct programs that efficiently exploit the power of today's multicore machines is hard. Structuring a program in such a way that parts can proceed in parallel is already non-trivial. However, if these parts belong to a single system, they inevitably will have to communicate and synchronize with each other. If two or more tasks (processes or threads) access the same data at the same time, these accesses *conflict*, unless they are all reads, in which case no communication will be achieved. If two conflicting accesses may happen concurrently, the program is said to allow a *data race*. As is consistent with Ada, C++, Java and C with Posix threads, such programs are generally considered erroneous.[1]

Programmers currently have to choose between one of two evils in order to synchronize accesses to shared data: use locks or atomic primitives, such as compare-and-swap. Neither provides the power, flexibility or robustness that are needed for real-time safety-critical systems. The use of atomic primitives, memory barriers or transactional memory are implementation details, that should not appear in actual user code [4].

When programmers use higher level synchronization primitives, like those provided by Java and Ada, only the implementations of these languages need to be enhanced to allow users to take advantage of the capabilities of current and upcoming hardware. While specified in terms of locks and mutual exclusion, we show that such monitor-like constructs constitute an excellent abstraction for both atomic primitives and transactional memory, allowing a compiler to automatically choose the best implementation for each target.

Section 2 will review the most widely used approaches to synchronization, which are typically implemented as a library. Next, Section 3 takes a closer look at language support for high-level synchronization constructs, and in particular the semantics of Ada's protected types. In Section 4, we introduce a new approach for implementing these protected types in a lock-free manner. Our experimental results in Section 5 show how this new implementation is not only safer, but also faster than the current lock-based implementation.

2. SYNCHRONIZATION LIBRARIES

2.1 Synchronization using Locks

Modern operating systems, such as GNU/Linux, use atomic primitives, such as compare-and-swap, to enable fast user-space implementations of locks that only require system calls when there is actual contention [5]. Any code using such locks directly or indirectly benefits from the atomic read-modify-write instructions provided by the hardware. However, using locks to provide mutual exclusion and protect

---

[1]The absence of data races as defined here does not imply that execution is deterministic, just that it is sequentially consistent and can be reasoned about. Similarly, in some cases there may be data races that can be shown to be harmless.

against concurrent updates of data-structures leads to new problems, such as: correct pairing, ordering, priority inversion and deadlock. Additionally, locks need correct initialization and finalization, which complicates their use in the presence of exceptions. For safety-critical embedded systems these problems are compounded, as it may not be safe to use locks from interrupt handlers.

Finally, there is the issue of serialization. Every lock is a potential bottleneck, especially if locks are potentially held for longer periods, either by design or as result of scheduling activity by the operating system. If 10% of a program's execution requires holding a specific lock, no amount of parallelism can ever result in more than a ten-fold speedup [1]. In particular, if a single lock protects multiple variables, the lock itself may cause a false conflict: two tasks using different variables may not execute concurrently as they require the same lock.

When the goal is to safely update a shared counter, and the system in fact has the capability to do so, it is not acceptable to have to use a lock. This is not only a matter of efficiency and scalability, but of correctness and robustness as well. Decisions on what synchronization methods to use depend on the target system and the context, such as scheduling priority of the task performing the operation, or whether run-time checks are required. When using libraries for synchronization, such decisions have to be explicit in the source code.

2.2 Synchronization using Atomic Primitives

The problems associated with library-based synchronization have long been known [3]. Still, current solutions for providing lock-free synchronization have focused on exposing the atomic primitives provided by the hardware directly, as a library API. The current C++ standard provides a large number of low-level synchronization primitives, and lets the programmer specify different forms of memory ordering. Java provides a similar library, though only supporting a sequentially consistent memory model.

While it certainly is possible to implement lock-free algorithms directly using atomic primitives, this approach is riddled with the same problems faced by programmers who were writing programs in terms of actual machine instructions at the dawn of the computer age. Writing programs this way is extremely time consuming, requires a deep understanding of low-level concepts and results in code that is needlessly specific to a particular hardware implementation. While one system may support atomic primitives for double precision floating point variables, another may not, requiring a different implementation approach.

Calling one of the C++ APIs for such an unsupported object may result in the implicit use of locks, with all of the associated problems. The function `atomic_is_lock_free` queries the lock-free property of an atomic object. The question is what to do if the query returns false. Unconditional use of the provided API can result in more locks and locking operations than if locks had been used directly at a higher level, but requiring users to provide two implementations for each synchronized operation is not reasonable either.

So, instead of simplifying the writing of correct programs, we argue that providing atomic primitives as a library hinders safe, simple and scalable synchronization. While often necessary at the implementation level, atomic primitives should not appear in portable user code.

3. SYNCHRONIZATION CONSTRUCTS

A few current programming languages support high level synchronization constructs. Java [6] has objects with synchronized methods and Ada [9] provides protected types. Both are based on the concept of *monitors* that originated in Concurrent Pascal [7]. Monitors contain a shared variable and their semantics are specified in terms of mutual exclusion, apparently implying the use of locks. While the language implementation ensures correct pairing of locking and unlocking, even in case of exceptions, most of the other drawbacks of explicit locking apply here as well, unfortunately.

Whenever two synchronized objects call on each other, there is a possibility for deadlock. Similarly, avoiding priority inversion remains hard on multi-processor systems. All tasks using a specific lock have to cooperate and establish a global protocol to avoid being cancelled or blocked due to preemption or further locking operations, while holding the lock.

While solving these problems in their entirety just by improving the language implementation is not currently feasible, a much restricted use of synchronized objects allows compilers to automatically determine a suitable lock-free implementation when possible. We will show that this gives the benefits of directly using atomic primitives, without incurring any of the drawbacks.

3.1 Semantics of Protected Objects

This section will focus on Ada's protected objects and show how an enhanced implementation of the language can provide an effective way to make certain data structures lock-free or wait-free, potentially even avoiding any locking or atomic primitives at all, automatically falling back to atomic primitives or locks where required and acceptable.

While for brevity only Ada is considered, similar approaches are possible for any programming language providing similar constructs, including Java. Protected objects with *entries*, that specify barriers, will not be considered, as calls on entries are by definition blocking operations.

```ada
protected Counter is
    procedure Increment;
    function  Get return Natural;
private
    Count : Natural := 0;
end Counter;


protected body Counter is
    procedure Increment is
    begin
        Count := Count + 1;
    end Increment;

    function Get return Natural is
    begin
        return Count;
    end Get;
end Counter;
```

Figure 1: Protected object implementing a simple counter

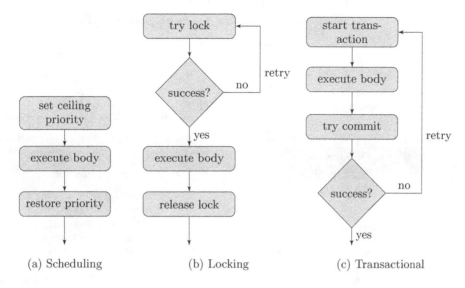

(a) Scheduling   (b) Locking   (c) Transactional

Figure 2: Possible Implementations of a Protected Action

Protected components are always private and can only be accessed through calls on protected procedures, which may perform updates, and functions, which only read. Together protected procedures and functions are referred to as *protected actions*.

In Ada, protected functions may execute concurrently with each other, but a protected procedure call is defined as acquiring the execution resources associated with a protected object for exclusive read-write access. In addition, two protected actions on the same protected object establish a sequential relationship between those actions, if at least one is a call on a protected procedure.

Protected actions may not execute delay statements, entry calls or other potentially blocking operations. A task trying to access a contended protected object is not considered to be blocked however, but is instead allowed to consume execution resources while waiting its turn. This allows both for the use of spinlocks, and efficient implementation of protected objects using speculative execution and transactional memory. See figure 2 for possible implementations.

3.2 Mutual Exclusion through Scheduling

Though the remainder of this chapter will focus on scaling up to larger multiprocessor systems, protected operations can also be implemented very efficiently on small embedded monoprocessor systems. Ada defines a first-in first-out scheduling protocol, named `FIFO_Within_Priorities`, where tasks can only be pre-empted by higher-priority tasks, as well as a `Ceiling_Locking` locking policy. With this policy, every protected object P has a priority ceiling associated with it. Tasks with a higher priority than that of P cannot call on P, while threads with a lower priority temporarily raise their priority to the ceiling priority.

While one task is executing a protected action on P, other tasks with a priority of at most P will not be able to execute until the protected action has completed. Thus, mutual exclusion is achieved by acquiring the execution resource (processor), without any need for the use of locking or atomic primitives. As a result this priority ceiling protocol guarantees freedom of priority inversion or deadlock [10].

4. TRANSACTIONAL IMPLEMENTATION OF PROTECTED ACTIONS

This section examines the ramifications of using a transactional approach for implementing protected actions, and the conditions under which this new technique meets the requirements of the language specification. Then we present our initial limited implementation, which even with all its restrictions has more capabilities than a fixed library of atomic primitives can have, while avoiding the problems inherent to a library-based approach.

4.1 Transactional Memory

A memory transaction is a finite sequence of operations on a shared memory, executed by a single task, that appears to execute both serially – not interleaved with operations from other tasks – and atomically. Each transaction makes a sequence of tentative changes to shared memory. When the transaction completes, it either commits, making all changes visible to all tasks instantaneously, or aborts. In this last case, all changes are discarded and never become visible to any other task [8]. Two transactions conflict if they cannot both be committed without potentially violating the serializability or atomicity requirements. In this case, when one transaction commits, the other one is doomed, as it will have to be aborted eventually.

While an application cannot in general detect the difference between speculatively executing the body of the protected operation or trying to acquire a spin lock, the maximum amount of time spent in a doomed transaction attempt must be bounded for this to be true. Similarly, a transaction may not execute any instructions that are observable by another task or have an external effect. These two limitations are the only fundamental restrictions on using memory transactions.

Practical implementations of transactional memory, in either hardware of software, have further limitations in both supported operations and capacity. As the determination whether a transactional approach is profitable for a certain program construct, is dependent on system details that may

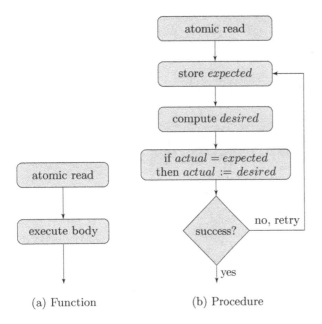

(a) Function   (b) Procedure

Figure 3: Minimal Implementation of Transactional Memory using Compare-and-Swap

change between target systems and over time, this choice should not be encoded in the program.

4.2 Minimalistic Implementation of Lock-free Protected Actions

New processor architectures, such as Intel's Haswell, will have support for sufficiently large transactions that many existing data structures using protected objects may be implemented using transactional memory. As our initial goal was to provide a better alternative to a fixed library of atomic primitives on the widest range of systems possible, we have decided to follow a minimalistic approach to memory transactions.

As protected components, such as `Count` in the example from figure 1, can only be accessed by protected actions of that type, it is possible for the compiler to analyze all code that may access the protected components and determine if the protected actions can be implemented as transactions. This allows the compiler to automatically choose between a lock-based or a transaction-based lock free implementation. Callers don't have to know the distinction and can make a regular function or procedure call in any case.

We require that memory transactions only access a single location in shared memory: the protected component. The atomic compare-and-swap compares the current value of a given memory location with an expected value, and if equal replaces it with the desired value computed by the body of the protected action. This allows a transaction to be implemented as shown in figure 3.

As it is common for protected procedures to only conditionally update a component, the compare-and-swap is omitted if both the expected and desired values are the same. In this case the procedure effectively has the same semantics as a protected function and its execution will be wait-free. This last property allows protected actions to implement objects with an infinite consensus number, see section 4.4.

4.3 Initial Restrictions on Protected Actions

For the initial implementation of lock-free protected objects, a number of constraints have been adopted:

1. To bound the time a speculatively executing transaction keeps executing after a conflicting transaction has been committed, the following Ada constructs are forbidden in lock-free protected actions:

   - loop, goto and procedure call statements
   - calls to non-static functions
   - quantified expressions

   Future implementations using transactional memory may be able to drop many or all of these limitations. Natural limits on transaction size or periodic interrupts or other events causing automatic aborts may bound the duration of a transaction. Then the challenge will be to make predictions, either at compile time or run time, of the profitability of speculative execution.

2. To restrict accesses to shared memory to a single location, a protected action can only refer to a single component, the size of which must not exceed the maximum size for which lock-free atomic primitives are supported. Additionally, the following are not allowed:

   - access to non-local variables (constants are fine)
   - non-elementary parameters
   - dereferences of access values (pointers)
   - address clauses
   - imported or exported entities
   - allocators (`new`)

3. To prevent instructions with external effect, volatile variables are not allowed.

None of the above restrictions are fundamental, and future implementations using transactional memory may eliminate most or all of them. Any objects not satisfying these constraints will use one of the other approaches given in figure 2. Given this list of restrictions, it is probably worth to mention that the handling and raising of exceptions is fine. In the procedure case, a raise statement still requires the transaction to be committed first. If the commit fails, the entire execution has to be redone as usual. Only when the commit succeeds will the raise statement be processed.

For exceptions raised as result of language defined checks, such as for overflow in integer arithmetic, Ada explicitly allows for raising an exception anywhere in the execution of the action, so no commit is necessary. From the user's point of view, such rollback is indeed better than leaving the protected object in a potentially inconsistent state.

4.4 Lock-free Protected Objects are Universal

Even with all of the restrictions in our initial implementation, lock-free protected objects turn out to be quite powerful. Consider the protected object in figure 4, implementing a compare-and-swap operation. This is in fact a wait-free compare-and-swap primitive. The loop generated by the compiler for the `Compare_And_Swap` procedure, see figure 3(b), can only iterate if `value = expected`, and in that case `expected` will change, causing the loop to exit. So, execution will always compete in bounded time.

```ada
protected Atomic_Integer is
   procedure Compare_And_Swap
      (Expected, Desired : Integer;
       Actual            : out Integer );
private
   Value : Integer;
end Atomic_Integer;

protected body Atomic_Integer is
   procedure Compare_And_Swap
      (Expected, Desired : Integer;
       Actual            : out Integer )
   is
   begin
      if Value = Expected then
         Value := Desired;
      end if;

      Actual := Value;
   end Compare_And_Swap;
end Atomic_Integer;
```

Figure 4: Protected object implementing compare-and-swap

4.5 Forcing a Lock-free Implementation

The GNAT Pro compiler associates a `Lock_Free` aspect (property) with each protected object. In addition to having the compiler automatically choose the best implementation, the programmer can set this aspect to be true. When specifying `with Lock_Free` or `with Lock_Free => True`, the compiler will avoid locks or give a compile-time error if this is not possible. When specifying `with Lock_Free => False`, the implementation will use explicit locking / unlocking calls. The attribute `'Lock_Free` can be used to query whether the actual implementation is indeed lock free.

Because generally an Ada program unit may only depend on the specification of other units, and not the implementation, callers of protected operations without `Lock_Free` aspect must assume they could be implemented using locks. Therefore, the protected object will include space for a lock, and initialization and finalization procedures must be called at appropriate points, even if the compiler ends up choosing a lock-free implementation. In that case the actual initialization and finalization will be null procedures, and the lock will remain unused.

By specifying the `Lock_Free` aspect in the specification, no space overhead is necessary. This allows a protected object to be as small as a single byte. Similarly, callers will know that no initialization and finalization is required. Protected objects can even be cheaper than simple atomic variables, because accesses may not require full barriers, as they are not defined to be synchronizing with other reads.

5. EXPERIMENTAL RESULTS

We have implemented the minimal approach shown in figure 3 in the GNAT Pro compiler. The GCC 4.7 back end, on which this compiler is based, provides the atomic primitives as compiler intrinsics. When these are not known at compile time to be lock-free, the compiler will complain if the `Lock_Free` aspect was specified, or otherwise fall back

Table 1: Implementations of the Simple Counter

Lock_Free aspect	False	True
Protected object size (bytes)	120	4
Mean time per update (ns)	132	24

on a lock-based implementation, if necessary. The compiler knows the semantic properties of its intrinsics, and will avoid code motion, speculation or other optimizations where needed.

5.1 Optimizing Opportunities

Because the lock-free code generation for protected objects does not require any library calls, and generally requires just a few instructions, all code can be inlined at the call sites. This means that synchronization instructions can be optimized in a similar fashion to regular computational code. In particular, consecutive memory barriers may be eliminated when the only instructions between them are known to not access potentially shared memory.

5.2 The Simple Counter

Going back to the example of the simple counter, it is worth mentioning that the lock-free compilation of this code includes all required Ada semantics, including overflow checking. A call to `Increment` that would cause an overflow situation does not lead to erroneous behavior or silent wraparound, but will raise a `Constraint_Error` exception, and leave the object in its unmodified state with the maximum possible value of `Count`.

When it can be proven that overflows cannot happen, or when the programmer requests these checks to be suppressed, the compiler may assume overflow cannot happen and optimize the code to an atomic increment, if such is provided by the target hardware. We have not implemented this optimization yet, but manual replacement of the generated code shows about a 15% improvement. Even using an unsafe, regular non-atomic increment instruction does not create a large speedup. Performance analysis shows that this is due to the cost of cache misses, which cannot be avoided.

For testing we use 4 tasks, each with its own protected counter. Of the increments, 90% are on the task's own counter, and 10% on the next task's counter. This means that there is a moderate amount of contention. All testing was done on a dual socket server with two Intel Xeon 5680 CPUs, each of which has 6 cores.

5.3 The Work Stealing Example

The work stealing algorithm is an efficient mechanism for scheduling a multi-threaded computation across a number of processors [2]. We have implemented a simple version of this algorithm with a bounded queue size. The head and tail indices are stored in a protected object. All queue operations are synchronized, and the only work done by a task of level n, is to update a processor-local task-counter and spawn n subtasks, one each for all $k \in \mathbb{N}$, with $0 \leq k < n$. While this represents a worst case, as no real computation is done and no attempt is made to reduce the number of synchronized operations, it has proven useful to find synchronization and fairness issues, and highlight the cost of the synchronization itself.

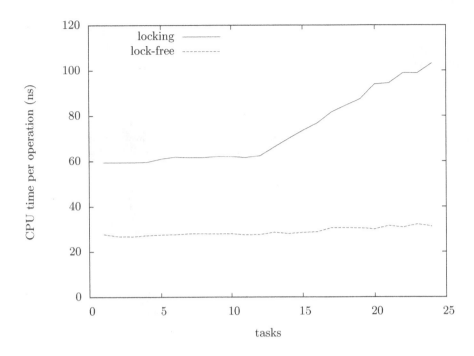

Figure 5: Cost of worklist operations

This test has low contention levels: each worker task generally services its own queue, and contention only arises if a task is idle and needs to steal work. While locking overhead in Linux is extremely low when there is little contention, the lock-free implementation using atomic primitives still yields a significant speedup. Even more important, the resulting code will not suffer priority inversion or deadlock.

Because of hyperthreading, our 12 core system appears as having 24 processors. To compute CPU time, we consider this system as a 24-processor system. In the graph, perfect scaling would mean the CPU usage per operation wouldn't change with more processors, resulting in a perfect horizontal line. Hyperthreading has no benefit for the implementation using locking, as with 24 tasks the per-operation cost doubles compared to the 12 tasks case. On the other hand, the lock-free implementation scaled nearly perfectly. A possible reason is that the much larger number of instructions and memory operations per iteration for the locking version already hits a resource bottleneck in the processor, while the lock free version does not.

6. CONCLUSION

Encouraging user applications to use libraries interfacing to low-level implementation specific facilities, such as atomic primitives or memory transactions, leads to inefficiency and overspecification. More importantly, when running programs on different hardware, performance may needlessly suffer, and implicit locking may lead to priority inversion, or even deadlock where none was expected. By using the right level of abstraction, programmers are freed from the need to understand low-level details about memory models and synchronization instructions, while compilers gain the freedom to use an optimal implementation based on target capabilities.

We have shown that it is possible to translate Ada's pro-

tected objects in a lock-free, or even wait-free manner using memory transactions or atomic primitives. Even with the large set of restrictions in our initial implementation, lock-free protected objects are more flexible and powerful than a fixed library of atomic primitives can be. By using high-level synchronized objects that allow users to specify the synchronization at the right level of abstraction, the same code can be used for systems ranging from small embedded microcontrollers to large multiprocessors with dozens of simultaneous threads. While additional implementation work is needed to lift the current restrictions and allow automatic use of more general forms of transactional memory for arbitary protected objects, the language is ready.

7. ACKNOWLEDGEMENTS

This project would not have been possible without the tireless help of Vincent Pucci, who did amazing work on the compiler, often implementing ideas as they hatched. I'd also like to thank the anonymous reviewers for their thoughtful comments.

8. REFERENCES

[1] AMDAHL, G. M. Validity of the single processor approach to achieving large scale computing capabilities. In *Proceedings of the April 18-20, 1967, spring joint computer conference* (New York, NY, USA, 1967), AFIPS '67 (Spring), ACM, pp. 483–485.

[2] BLUMOFE, R. D., AND LEISERSON, C. E. Scheduling multithreaded computations by work stealing. *J. ACM 46*, 5 (Sept. 1999), 720–748.

[3] BOEHM, H.-J. Threads cannot be implemented as a library. *SIGPLAN Not. 40*, 6 (June 2005), 261–268.

[4] BOEHM, H.-J. Transactional memory should be an implementation technique, not a programming

interface. In *Proceedings of the First USENIX conference on Hot topics in parallelism* (Berkeley, CA, USA, 2009), HotPar'09, USENIX Association, pp. 15–15.

[5] FRANKE, H., RUSSELL, R., AND FUSS, M. K. futexes and furwocks: Fast userlevel locking in linux. In *Proceedings of the 2002 Ottawa Linux Summit* (2002), Ottawa Linux Symposium 2002, pp. 479–495.

[6] GOSLING, J., JOY, B., STEELE, G., AND BRACHA, G. *Java(TM) Language Specification, The (3rd Edition) (Java (Addison-Wesley))*. Addison-Wesley Professional, 2005.

[7] HANSEN, P. B. History of programming languages—ii. ACM, New York, NY, USA, 1996, ch. Monitors and Concurrent Pascal: a personal history, pp. 121–172.

[8] HERLIHY, M., AND MOSS, J. E. B. Transactional memory: architectural support for lock-free data structures. *SIGARCH Comput. Archit. News 21*, 2 (May 1993), 289–300.

[9] TAFT, S. T., DUFF, R. A., BRUKARDT, R. L., PLOEDEREDER, E., AND LEROY, P. *Ada 2005 Reference Manual. Language and Standard Libraries: International Standard ISO/IEC 8652/1995(E) with Technical Corrigendum 1 and Amendment 1 (Lecture Notes in Computer Science)*. Springer-Verlag New York, Inc., Secaucus, NJ, USA, 2007.

[10] YUE, K.-B., DAVARI, S., AND LEIBFRIED, T. Priority ceiling protocol in ada. In *Proceedings of the conference on TRI-Ada '96: disciplined software development with Ada* (New York, NY, USA, 1996), TRI-Ada '96, ACM, pp. 3–9.

Applicability of Real-Time Schedulability Analysis on a Software Radio Protocol

Shuai Li+*, Frank Singhoff*, Stéphane Rubini*, Michel Bourdellès+

+THALES Communications & Security, 4 Avenue des Louvresses, 92622 Gennevilliers, France
*Lab-STICC/UMR 6285, UBO, UEB, 20 Avenue Le Gorgeu, 29200 Brest, France
{shuai.li,michel.bourdelles}@fr.thalesgroup.com, {rubini,singhoff}@univ-brest.fr

ABSTRACT

In this paper, we present our experience on integrating timing constraint verification and analysis, by using the real-time scheduling theory, in an industrial context. The verification process has been integrated into a design flow at THALES Communications & Security. We focus our work on Software Radio Protocols (SRP). We have used Model-Driven Engineering technologies and the Cheddar schedulability analysis tool for our experiment. We show how we have modeled a complete SRP in UML MARTE, a profile for real-time embedded systems, before using model transformation to extract information for schedulability analysis with Cheddar.

Categories and Subject Descriptors

D2.4 [**Software Engineering**]: Software/Program Verification— *Validation*

General Terms

Performance, Reliability, Verification

Keywords

Real-Time Embedded System, Software Radio Protocol, Real-Time Scheduling, Non-Functional Properties, Model-Driven Engineering, UML, MARTE

1. INTRODUCTION

In this paper, we explore the modeling and the schedulability analysis of a Software Radio Protocol (SRP).

A SRP is a Real-Time Embedded System (RTES) in the telecommunication domain. As a RTES, a SRP has timing constraints. Schedulability analysis is thus necessary. This analysis is done by using the real-time scheduling theory.

This theory dates back to the 70s with the seminal Liu and Layland work [17]. Although the real-time scheduling theory is mature [36] the breakthrough in the industry is

not significant [39]. We believe this reluctance is due to the lack of domain-specific guidelines for system engineers. Even though tools exist to ease RTES' schedulability analysis, we believe they must be integrated directly into the domain-specific design tools. Developing bridges between the design tools and the analysis tools is one such possibility to accomplish this goal.

In this paper we study the applicability of the real-time scheduling theory on a SRP. In our solution, we use models coupled with schedulability analysis tools. Modeling and Analysis of Real Time Embedded systems (MARTE) [26] is a UML profile dedicated to RTES analysis. Cheddar [38] is a real-time schedulability analysis tool based on feasibility tests and simulation. We present our work on SRP modeling in MARTE and its analysis with Cheddar. We see how this process can be integrated into an industrial design flow at THALES Communications & Security (TCS), based on a Model-Driven Engineering (MDE) approach [34].

The rest of the article is organized as follows. Some related works are presented in section 2. Section 3 exposes our work's context. Section 4 presents the SRP architecture properties for schedulability analysis. Section 5 lists the modeling and schedulability analysis requirements on our work. SRP modeling with MARTE is shown in section 6. Section 7 presents the Cheddar scheduling analysis tool. The mapping between a SRP MARTE model and Cheddar is given in section 8. The suggested solution is experimented on a SRP application in section 9 and we also give its evaluation in this section. Finally we conclude in section 10 and we list some future works.

2. RELATED WORKS

System performance analysis, and particularly schedulability analysis, has been extensively studied in the literature. The analysis flows that interest us consist of modeling the system with an Architecture Description Language (ADL) [20] and analyzing it with a schedulability analysis tool.

In [8], a system modeled in the Architecture Analysis & Design Language (AADL) [9] is analyzed with Cheddar. AADL is derived from MetaH and it is possible to model both the software and hardware architecture of a RTES with this modeling language. Although AADL has been defined as a generic ADL, it is mostly used in the avionic domain due to its historical origins.

In [16], the authors explore timing analysis with an AUTO-SAR-based [3] modeling language. The commercial SymTA/S [44] analysis tool is used for schedulability analysis. SymTA/S is based on compositional scheduling. Although less accurate in some cases, since its does not have a global view of the system, this technique is well adapted to system scalability [12]. The AUTOSAR ADL is dedicated to the automotive world. At the same time SymTA/S is tuned for the automotive industry, supporting typical domain specific buses like CAN or FlexRay.

EAST-ADL2 [7] has been extended with MARTE for schedulability analysis. Although the domain-specific language EAST-ADL2 uses a generic modeling language like MARTE for its schedulability analysis extensions, the suggested approach is applied on automotive systems.

Other works bridge MARTE system models with schedulability analysis tools.

RapidRMA [13] is a tool developed and commercialized by Tri-pacific Software. It is integrated into IBM's Rational Software Architect (RSA) [42] which supports the MARTE profile. In the RapidRMA model, software resources are mapped onto hardware resources. The analysis tool features rate monotonic and deadline monotonic analysis [17].

Experimentation on using MARTE for schedulability analysis has been done through the MARTE to MAST [19] transformation tool. MAST [11] is an open-source schedulability analysis tool developed by the University of Cantabria. MAST allows to verify if the system will meet its timing requirements while also offering the possibility to see how close the system is to meeting these requirements. MAST main features are worst-case response time analysis, blocking time calculation, sensitivity analysis, and optimized priority assignment techniques. The MARTE model for MAST focuses on activity diagrams, transactions and activity triggers. This is well suited for end-to-end flow analysis [47].

As explained in section 6, our MARTE model is different from the MARTE model used for MAST. We describe the architecture and we map it to resources. This is similar to the Rapid-RMA approach.

To our knowledge, no work has been done on the applicability of a MARTE/Cheddar-based approach for schedulability analysis in the specific SRP domain.

In the following sections we present the current modeling technologies and we characterize the SRP system in order to establish requirements on the modeling language and schedulability analysis tool.

3. CONTEXT OF THE WORK

The current modeling language used at THALES Communications & Security for SRP development is MyCCM [46], an implementation of the CORBA Component Model (CCM) [23]. MyCCM uses a component-based approach. The SRP is modeled as inter-connected components that communicate through their ports implementing an interface. In MyCCM, it is possible to define a deployment plan by allocating the functional components onto threads and processes. The model is used to generate wrapper code for the components, i.e. Interface Definition Language (IDL) files and Component Deployment Plan (CDP) files. PrismTech proposes solutions for CCM (SpectraCX [31]) and the modelers are used at THALES. This model-driven development tool is built above the Eclipse framework.

The SRP modeling guideline for schedulability analysis suggested in this paper, is based on the European ITEA project Validation-drivEn design foR component-baseD architEctures (VERDE) [48]. We use in particular the functional entities modeling from VERDE. Figure 1 highlights

the analysis parts in VERDE that we have adapted for Cheddar. In this figure our contribution concerns the schedulability analysis.

4. SOFTWARE RADIO PROTOCOL

A Software Radio Protocol (SRP) is a radio protocol embedded in a radio equipment. A SRP is composed of one or several applications called waveforms that are running on a platform.

A waveform is composed of different software components that manage radio channel access technologies, radio protocol and routing. The waveform design may be separated into several functional layers following coarsely the OSI model [50]:

- PHY: Synchronization, data transmission/reception

- LINK: Protocol management

- NET: User packet handling

The platform offers services to the waveform. The platform is composed of:

- the Operating System (OS)

- the Hardware (HW)

Since the waveform is generally developed independently of the platform for interoperability issues, a waveform's performance analysis must be carried out on each platform. Performance analysis must investigate timing constraints and processor utilization.

In the next paragraphs we establish a list of the entities composing a SRP's waveform and platform. We also characterize the SRP's architecture from a schedulability analysis point of view.

4.1 Entities of a SRP

The SRP entities have been gathered into three groups: functional entities, OS entities and hardware entities.

4.1.1 Functional entities

The waveform is composed of functional entities which are the following:

Functional Component A set of functionalities and services that can be connected with other components sharing its interfaces.

Port A component's port is the entry-point for other components. Through a port a component requires or provides services. A port is typed with an interface.

Interface An interface regroups operations. Operations are the services and functionalities implemented by the component.

Datatype and Enumeration Operations have parameters that are typed by Datatypes, Primitives (a specific type of Datatype), and Enumerations.

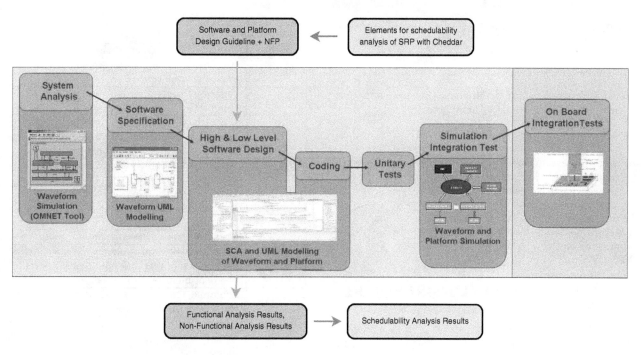

Figure 1: Contribution to THALES Communications & Security Design Flow

4.1.2 Operating system entities

OS entities are elements composing the runtime for the waveforms. These entities are executable software units, memory spaces, critical resources, and their managers. The OS entities needed for analysis are:

Thread A software unit of execution in the OS.

Process Threads are allocated onto processes. While being a unit of execution itself, a process is defined as a memory space in our work.

Scheduler The different units of execution are scheduled according to a policy defined by the scheduler in the OS. Note that several schedulers may be present in the model.

Shared Resource A shared resource is one that is accessed concurrently by different units of execution. They are protected with a protocol implemented in the OS.

Buffer A buffer is a resource used in the producer/consumer pattern. E.g. one thread writes periodically into a FIFO buffer while another thread reads periodically from it.

4.1.3 Hardware entities

Key hardware resources also need to be identified for the analysis tools. The degree of details of the hardware model also depends on the schedulability analysis tool. In a first step, we consider a simple hardware model composed of the following entities:

Processor The Central Processing Unit (CPU) is a key element in the platform model as it executes the threads.

Core A core is a computing resource. A processor may contain one or several cores (monocore and multicore processors).

Cache A cache is a memory shared by processors and cores. L1 caches are shared by cores and L2 caches are shared by processors.

4.2 Architecture Properties for Schedulability Analysis

Several works have been done on schedulability analysis at the PHY layer [45]. Threads have a periodic nature and the application is a signal processing one. With such properties, the analysis is made much more easier because signal processing and multimedia applications can be abstracted as data-flow applications. Unfortunately what stands true at the PHY layer is not necessarily true at LINK and NET layers. The architecture properties related to schedulability analysis are:

Heterogeneous Platforms SRP platforms are heterogeneous and threads run on different partitions, on different processors. This partitioning is due, in particular, to security issues (separation of critical and non-critical data) [5].

Scheduling Policy Scheduling policies are fixed priority-based and preemptive for the LINK and NET layers.

Execution time Execution times are variable and non-cyclic. E.g. Quality of Service (QoS) and the state in which the system is, influence the threads' execution time.

Thread Activation Pattern Not all threads in the LINK and NET layers are triggered periodically. Some threads may also be activated on event arrival. Threads may have a latency between its activation and its real execution. Threads in the system are not necessarily activated at the same time.

Thread Deadline Some threads are activated periodically but their execution may span over several periods, e.g. non-critical threads for radio stations synchronization.

Data flow and control flow Several data and control flows transit in the system, going through several functional components. Verifying that these flows finish before a defined deadline is a key issue.

Thread communication Communication between threads may be synchronous or asynchronous.

Resource Standard protocols (e.g. PCP, PIP [37]) for mutual exclusion are used to protect shared resources access between threads. This depends on the used platform and the protocols may not be used or implemented on certain platforms.

Following our work's context presented in section 3 and the SRP presentation in section 4, we have established the requirements on the modeling and schedulability analysis of a SRP.

5. MODELING AND ANALYSIS REQUIREMENTS

Table 1 lists the modeling requirements. These modeling requirements meet the current software engineering practices at THALES, extended with the modeling of elements required for schedulability analysis. Table 2 lists the schedulability tool requirements.

Table 1: Modeling Requirements

Ref.	Description
MREQ1	Component-based model: Due to the nature of MyCCM, the waveform and platform models are designed with a component approach.
MREQ2	Modular platform model: Platform entities must be separated into several layers for modularity.
MREQ3	Push-button logic: The proposed schedulability analysis method must not need extended expertise in the real-time scheduling theory.

6. MODELING A SRP WITH MARTE

In the previous sections, we exposed the modeling context of the work, the architecture entities and its schedulability properties. We now present our contribution on SRP modeling for schedulability analysis with the UML MARTE profile.

A UML profile is a mechanism that extends UML for a specific domain. As a profile is a generic extension of the base modeling language, it does not contradict the original language's semantics. Concretely, a UML profile is implemented as a set of stereotypes, tag values, and constraints applied to elements inside UML, e.g. classes, operations, activities, interactions. A stereotype is a mechanism to extend the UML vocabulary by defining a UML element as something specific for a domain, with specific attributes.

The MARTE UML profile extends UML to add support for modeling elements and concepts that are specific to RTES. The MARTE profile is composed of several sub-profiles to represent different concepts of a RTES at different levels of abstraction of the real system.

Table 2: Schedulability Analysis Tool Requirements

Ref.	Description
SREQ1	Heterogeneous multiprocessor platforms must be supported.
SREQ2	Processor context switch overhead must be supported.
SREQ3	Hierarchical scheduling must be supported. Spatial distribution (allocation of threads on processes on processors) must be supported.
SREQ4	Highest Priority First scheduling policies must be implemented.
SREQ5	User can express specific schedulers.
SREQ6	Specific priorities assignment can be implemented.
SREQ7	User can express specific thread parameters.
SREQ8	Variable execution times can be specified.
SREQ9	Periodic, sporadic and aperiodic dispatching protocol must be supported.
SREQ10	Dynamic/static jitters and offsets for task release time must be supported [27].
SREQ11	User can express specific thread release time.
SREQ12	User can assign any values for thread deadlines.
SREQ13	End-to-end timing analysis must be implemented.
SREQ14	Thread precedencies must be supported.
SREQ15	Blocking and non-blocking communications must be supported.
SREQ16	Shared resources between threads must be supported.
SREQ17	Standard shared resource protocols must be implemented.
SREQ18	Resource access duration by threads can be specified.

As MARTE is a big profile, with scarce guidelines for the designer [2] [32], it can become confusing to decide how to model a system in MARTE. Especially since many methods are possible and best practices are not always evident. It is thus important to define a guideline to model the RTES with MARTE for a specific kind of analysis. MARTE acts as a framework to define the modeling guideline.

In section 4.1, we have decided to separate the entities into three categories: the functional waveform, the OS, and the hardware. Figure 2 gives the corresponding model packages. In the following paragraphs we expose our guideline for modeling the entities with MARTE sub-profiles. The sub-profiles are presented first before we show how we use them. The associations between the different entities are also explained at the end.

6.1 Waveform Modeling

The Generic Component Model (GCM) sub-profile addresses designer needs in applying the component-based model paradigm. Its main contribution to our model relies in the annotations it provides to model the component's ports.

High Level Application Model (HLAM) is a sub-profile that provides designer with facilities to annotate their model to represent high level artifacts such as set of functionalities in a block.

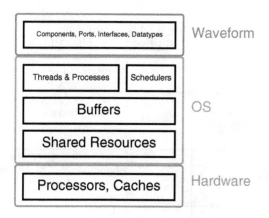

Figure 2: Model Packages

Figure 3 describes the stereotypes in the GCM and HLAM sub-profiles that we have used.

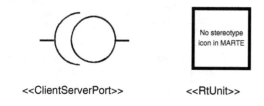

<<ClientServerPort>>   <<RtUnit>>

Figure 3: Applied GCM and HLAM Stereotypes

Table 3 maps the different functional entities to their stereotyped UML elements in MARTE.

Table 3: Waveform Modeling in UML and MARTE

Functional Entity	MARTE Model
Functional Component	**Component** stereotyped $\langle\langle RtUnit\rangle\rangle$ from **HLAM**
Port	**Port** stereotyped $\langle\langle ClientServerPort\rangle\rangle$ from **GCM**
Interface	**Class** stereotyped $\langle\langle Interface\rangle\rangle$ from **UML**
Datatype	**Class** stereotyped $\langle\langle Datatype\rangle\rangle$ from **UML**
Enumeration	**Enumeration** from **UML**

6.2 Operating System Modeling

The General Resource Modeling (GRM) and Software Resource Modeling (SRM) sub-profiles have been used to model the OS entities. GRM enables execution platform modeling and provides the foundations needed for a more refined modeling of both hardware (Hardware Resource Modeling) and software (Software Resource Modeling) resources.

Designing a multitasking application is based on a Real-Time Operating System (RTOS) that offers resources through Application Programming Interfaces (API). The SRM sub-profile offers artifacts to model the support provided by the RTOS, i.e. its API. SRM has been built upon observing elements present in several standard RTOS API (POSIX, OSEK/VDX, ARINC 653) and RTOS (VxWorks, RTAI, QNX).

Figure 4 enumerates the GRM and SRM stereotypes used in the OS resources modeling.

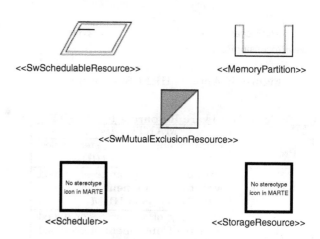

<<SwSchedulableResource>>   <<MemoryPartition>>

<<SwMutualExclusionResource>>

<<Scheduler>>   <<StorageResource>>

Figure 4: Applied GRM and SRM Stereotypes

Table 4 maps the different OS resources to their stereotyped UML elements in MARTE.

Table 4: OS Entities to MARTE

OS Entity	MARTE Model
Thread	**Component** stereotyped $\langle\langle SwSchedulableResource\rangle\rangle$ from **SRM**
Process	**Component** stereotyped $\langle\langle MemoryPartition\rangle\rangle$ from **SRM**
Shared Resource	**Class** stereotyped $\langle\langle SwMutualExclusionResource\rangle\rangle$ from **SRM**
Buffer	**Component** stereotyped $\langle\langle StorageResource\rangle\rangle$ from **GRM**
Scheduler	**Component** stereotyped $\langle\langle Scheduler\rangle\rangle$ from **GRM**

6.3 Hardware Modeling

The Hardware Resource Modeling (HRM) sub-profile has been used to model hardware entities. The HRM sub-profile provides several stereotypes to model the platform hardware through three different views: a high-level architectural view, a specialized view and a detailed physical view. We have decided to stay at a high-level architectural view with enough annotations needed for analysis. This is because our goal is to have a first estimation of the application's performance on a platform, without the need for the system engineer to supply too much detail on the hardware components.

Figure 5 enumerates the stereotypes in the HRM sub-profile needed for our model.

Table 5 maps the different hardware resources to their stereotyped UML elements in MARTE.

6.4 Associations Between Entities

Specific UML associations (e.g. Abstraction, Usage) stereotyped with MARTE are used to represent the relationships between the entities of each category. Each association has

<<HwProcessor>>
<<HwProcessingResource>>

<<HwCache>>

Figure 5: Applied HRM Stereotypes

Table 5: Hardware Resources to MARTE

HW Entity	MARTE Model
Processor	**Component** stereotyped $\langle\langle HwProcessor \rangle\rangle$ from **HRM**
L2 Cache	**Property** of the processor typed with the **Component** stereotyped $\langle\langle HwCache \rangle\rangle$ from **HRM**
Core	**Property** of the processor typed with the **Component** stereotyped $\langle\langle HwComputingResource \rangle\rangle$ from **HRM**
L1 Cache	**Property** of the core typed with the **Component** stereotyped $\langle\langle HwCache \rangle\rangle$ from **HRM**

a client and a supplier depending on the role of each end. UML interactions are also used to represent the relationships, which are shown in different views:

Spatial Distribution View The spatial distribution view links the functional entities to the OS entities and the OS entities to the hardware entities. Concretely the spatial distribution view shows how entities at different levels are allocated onto one another. An allocation is a UML Abstraction stereotyped $\langle\langle Allocate \rangle\rangle$ from MARTE. The UML Abstraction has a client (the element that is allocated) and a supplier (the element that is allocated onto). The different possible allocations are listed in Table 6.

Critical Resource Usage View The critical resource usage view shows how threads use shared resources and buffers. A resource usage is a UML Usage stereotyped $\langle\langle ResourceUsage \rangle\rangle$ from the MARTE GRM subprofile. The UML Usage has a client (the resource user) and a supplier (the resource used). Through the $\langle\langle ResourceUsage \rangle\rangle$ stereotype, we can specify the resource usage time. We use a UML Constraint stereotyped $\langle\langle TimedConstraint \rangle\rangle$ from the MARTE Time sub-profile to specify the resource usage start time in the thread's execution time. The UML Constraint constrains the UML Usage.

Dependency View Communications between entities are represented through a dependency view that is a communication diagram in UML. In the communication diagram, a UML Lifelines represents a thread or a buffer. A dependency is established between two entities if there is a UML Message between the two UML Lifelines representing the entities. The direction of the message matters while establishing the dependent and dependable roles.

Table 6: Allocations

Client	Supplier	Description
Component	Thread	The functional component contains a thread triggered by events.
Port	Thread	The port's operations are handled by a thread triggered by calls to any of the operations.
Operation	Thread	A specific operation is handled by a thread triggered by a call to the operation.
Thread	Process	A thread is executed in the context of a memory partition (process).
Shared Resource	Process	A shared resource is located in a memory partition.
Buffer	Process	A buffer is located in a memory partition.
Process	Processor	The threads of a process are executed on a processor. At least one process exists for each processor.

7. CHEDDAR, AN ADA SCHEDULABILITY ANALYSIS TOOL

Cheddar is an open-source schedulability and timing constraints analysis tool developed and maintained by the University of Western Brittany/Lab-STICC since 2001. From 2008 and onward, Ellidiss Technologies participates in the tool's industrial distribution by providing industrial support [8].

System and architecture models can be analyzed in Cheddar using the AADL standard or the tool's own design language. The Cheddar analysis environment includes two main elements: a graphical editor and a core analysis framework. The graphical editor helps the designer to describe the real-time system architecture to be analyzed. The core analysis framework includes the different scheduling algorithms, feasibility tests, and analysis found in the real-time scheduling literature.

The core analysis framework is composed of a simulation engine and a feasibility tests analyzer. It can be seen as a library of tests and analysis methods that the designer can choose to verify timing constraints.

When no analysis is applicable to a system's task model and scheduling policy, this does not mean that important properties of the system cannot be found, e.g. the system's non-schedulability. The Cheddar simulator provides features for these kind of systems. Furthermore the simulator can be coupled with another one of Cheddar's key feature: the modeling of user-defined parameters for tasks and the implementation of user-defined schedulers. The system can then be analyzed by simulations.

Cheddar is partly generated from a meta-model with a model-driven process [30]. The Cheddar meta-model is defined in EXPRESS [24], a modeling language. Figure 6 shows the Cheddar meta-model. For the sake of space and clarity, class properties and child classes are not present in the diagram. Cheddar is implemented in Ada and runs on Unix-based OS (Solaris, Debian Linux) and Windows.

From the Cheddar model, we have defined the transformation rules between MARTE and Cheddar in the following section.

8. MARTE TO CHEDDAR TRANSFORMATION

Model transformation [35] is part of MDE and it ensures the consistency between different models. In model transformation an appropriate model (i.e. conform to the input meta-model) is used as input for the transformation tool. The tool's output is a model conform to the output meta-model. The output model represents complementary information of the system on a different level, in a different view or for a different use.

Our work is based on the first transformation [18] developed by THALES. This transformation was implemented as a IBM RSA plug-in. Several Cheddar entities are not taken into account in this work (e.g. multicore processor) and we have modified it for SRP analysis.

Table 7 lists the mapping of MARTE entities to Cheddar entities.

Table 7: MARTE to Cheddar Mapping

MARTE	Cheddar
$\langle\langle HwProcessor \rangle\rangle$	Processor
$\langle\langle HwProcessingResource \rangle\rangle$	Core_Unit
$\langle\langle HwCache \rangle\rangle$	Cache
Properties typed $\langle\langle HwCache \rangle\rangle$	Cache_System
$\langle\langle Scheduler \rangle\rangle$	Scheduler
$\langle\langle MemoryPartition \rangle\rangle$	Address_Space
$\langle\langle StorageResource \rangle\rangle$	Buffer
$\langle\langle SwMutualExclusionResource \rangle\rangle$	Resource
$\langle\langle SwSchedulableResource \rangle\rangle$	Task
$\langle\langle Allocation \rangle\rangle$	Address_Space_Name property of Task, Resource, Buffer. Cpu_Name property of Address_Space, Task, Resource, Buffer
$\langle\langle ResourceUsage \rangle\rangle$	Task_Tab property of Resource (list of tasks using the resource). Roles property of Buffer (list of roles for the buffer)
$\langle\langle GaScenario \rangle\rangle$'s Message (UML)	Dependency

The MARTE to Cheddar transformation has been implemented as an Eclipse plug-in using the Papyrus [28] modeler and its MARTE implementation. The size of the Eclipse modeling ecosystem is large, with numerous tools and modelers implemented using the Eclipse Modeling Framework (EMF) [41], [28], [42], [6], [40]. Industrial modeling tools like SpectraCX [31] are also built upon Eclipse. We choose an Eclipse-based implementation for integration with tools used at THALES. Experiments on the system's modeling

and transformation to Cheddar are presented in the following section.

9. EXPERIMENT

In order to test our SRP schedulability analysis method in an industrial context, we decided to experiment with a system's simulation developed at THALES.

9.1 Software Radio Protocol Case-Study

The IP TDMA-Based Protocol (ITBP) protocol has been designed to expose and demonstrate the main constraints encountered in modern protocols designed at THALES. ITBP is IP-based and uses Time Division Multiple Access (TDMA) [4] for radio channel separation. In TDMA, time is divided into several time slots. At each slot a station has an action to perform and the mapping between the actions and the time slots is called a TDMA allocation. As explained in section 4, the system's waveform design follows the OSI model. Figure 7 shows the different layers in the waveform.

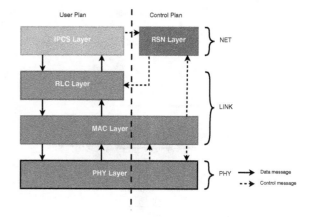

Figure 7: ITBP Layers and Sub-layers

Several data (Protocol Data Unit (PDU)) and control flows transit through the waveform's different layers. The data and control flows depend on the type of the time slot being processed, and the system's state. Under the experimental conditions, the waveform's functional behavior is the following:

1. IP Packets arrive from the IP stack and are segmented into RLC PDU before being stored in the RLC layer.

2. RLC PDU are handled and segmented into MAC PDU before being stored in the MAC.

3. A tick from synchronization source (e.g. GPS) indicates the start of a new slot.

4. The current slot type and next one are checked according to the slots allocation.

5. PDU stored in the MAC is passed to the PHY for transmission over air on the next slot.

6. Received data is transferred from the PHY to the IPCS.

7. The system is prepared for the next slot.

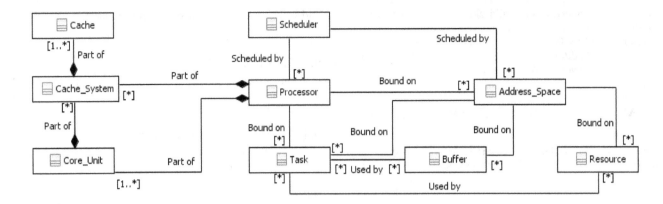

Figure 6: Cheddar Meta-Model

The waveform is deployed on a platform with five threads. Figure 8 summarizes the threads' shared resources and communication dependencies. The threads' detailed properties are given in table 8. Table 9 shows the shared resources and their usage. The shared resources are protected by Linux's default FIFO mutex protocol, i.e. there is not protection against priority inversion [37].

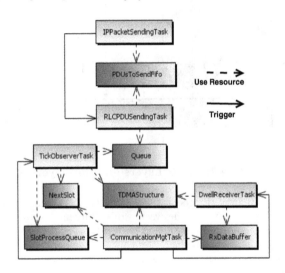

Figure 8: ITBP Threads and Resources Dependencies

IPPacketSendingTask This thread reads from the IP stack and transmits packets to the *PDUsToSendFifo*. All station routes to other stations have already been established previously.

RLCPDUSendingTask This thread is awaken by the *IPPacketSendingTask*, each time there are data in the *PDUsToSendFifo*. It segments the PDU and transmits them to the *Queue*.

CommunicationManagementTask[1] This thread is activated by a tick from the exterior synchronization source. It processes the current slot and verifies its

[1]May be abbreviated as "CommMgtTask" for the rest of this paper.

correctness by checking the *TDMAStructure*. Afterwards it updates *NextSlot* with the next slot id, and wakes the *TickObserverTask* thread. On reception it stores received data in the *RxDataBuffer*. All slot allocations are static for the experiment.

TickObserverTask[2] This thread is awaken by the *CommunicationManagementTask*. It reads *NextSlot* and configures PHY for the next slot. It also transmits the data to be send over air on the next slot (stored originally in the *Queue*) to the *SlotProcessQueue*. The *TDMAStructure* is checked for slot consistency. These operations have to be done before the next slot.

DwellReceiverTask This thread is awaken by the *CommunicationManagementTask*, each time there are data in the *RxDataBuffer*. It processes the data and sends it to the IP stack. The *TDMAStructure* is checked for slot consistency.

9.2 Experiment Setup

The setup for the ITBP simulation that we have used to study its schedulability is shown in figure 9.

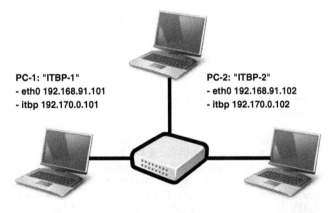

Figure 9: Experiment Setup

[2]May be abbreviated as "TickObs" for the rest of this paper.

Table 8: ITBP Threads Properties

Thread	Property	Value
IPPacketSendingTask	Activation	Sporadic
	Inter-arrival	$6000\mu s$
	Priority	20
	Capacity	$207\mu s$
	Deadline	None
RLCPDUSendingTask	Activation	Sporadic
	Inter-arrival	$6000\mu s$
	Priority	10
	Capacity	$1725\mu s$
	Deadline	None
TickObserverTask	Activation	Periodic
	Period	$5000\mu s$
	Priority	10
	Capacity	$773\mu s$
	Deadline	$5000\mu s$
DwellReceiverTask	Activation	Sporadic
	Inter-arrival	$10000\mu s$
	Priority	10
	Capacity	$917\mu s$
	Deadline	None
CommMgtTask	Activation	Periodic
	Period	$5000\mu s$
	Priority	40
	Capacity	$1115\mu s$
	Deadline	$5000\mu s$

Table 9: ITBP Shared Resources

Resource	Used by	Start (μs)	End (μs)
PDUsToSendFifo	IPPacketSendingTask	30	34
	RLCPDUSendingTask	1	3
Queue	RLCPDUSendingTask	127	1624
	TickObserverTask	16	142
TDMAStructure	DwellReceiverTask	65	67
	TickObserverTask	4	6
	CommMgtTask	109	111
RxDataBuffer	DwellReceiverTask	1	27
	CommMgtTask	93	107
NextSlot	TickObserverTask	0	772
	CommMgtTask	329	330
SlotProcessQueue	TickObserverTask	84	90
	CommMgtTask	0	325
	CommMgtTask	708	758

Three PC are connected through a central hub. PC-1 and PC-2 each run a ITBP protocol while PC-3 (called the "Communication Server") plays the role of a network clock, i.e. it broadcasts ticks to PC-1 and PC-2. PC-3 also manages data routing, i.e. PC-1 and PC-2 send their packets to PC-3 which redirects the packets to the correct station.

On PC-1 and PC-2 the ITBP protocol is launched as a virtual network interface (called *itbp*) that reads packets coming from the main *eth0* interface. The packets coming from *eth0* are in the ITBP proprietary format. An user application reads the assembled IP packets from the virtual *itbp* interface by using the virtual address 192.170.0.x. It also sends user data to another station by sending to a virtual address. For our experiment we used VLC [49] to stream a video between PC-1 and PC-2.

The ITBP protocol is run on a quad-core PC with Ubuntu Linux. At start up, the *taskset* command is used to set the PID 1 process core-affinity to 0-2. This core-affinity is inherited by all child processes spawn by process 1. Core 3 is then available to run ITBP alone. Only system processes still persist on core 3 as these processes are duplicated on all cores during kernel boot.

The ITBP threads are POSIX threads with properties SCHED_FIFO and PTHREAD_SCOPE_SYSTEM. The first property ensures that the threads are scheduled with a fixed priority-based scheduler, i.e. they can only be preempted by other SCHED_FIFO threads and system threads. By setting the threads' scope to system scope, they are scheduled as system threads.

9.3 MARTE Model

The system's MARTE model's diagrams are shown in the appendix section. With respect to section 6, the waveform

has been modeled as inter-connected components in UML MARTE. Figure 14 gives a cut view of the MAC sub-layer.

Figure 15 shows the spatial distribution view with elements present in the execution platform (OS and hardware).

Figure 12 shows the shared resource usage by the threads.

Figure 13 shows the threads communication dependencies through the UML communication diagram.

9.4 Analysis Evaluation

In the following sections we present and analyze three significant results given by the conducted experiment. In order to evaluate Cheddar's analysis results on the described system, we used execution trace coming from code instrumentation [3].

9.4.1 Software Design Mistake

A first analysis was done by injecting the data in table 8 directly into the MARTE model and generating the matching Cheddar model. A model where all threads are periodic (sporadic threads are abstracted as periodic threads), start at the same time, and run at their full capacity (WCET), is generated. With this model, feasibility tests based on processor utilization and response time can be done. Table 10 shows the Worst Case Response Time (WCRT) given by Cheddar through feasibility tests. Figure 10 shows the measured response times distribution for *CommunicationManagementTask* and *TickObserverTask* (the threads with deadlines). When comparing the results, we see that the *TickObserverTask* exceeds the predictions. Note that the small *IPPacketSendingTask* measured response time is explained by the fact that we did not instrument system functions so we could not capture the exact arrival of an IP packet. As this thread does not have a hard deadline, this issue is not important for our experiment.

This difference can be explained by a software design mistake. The *CommunicationManagementTask*'s inactive time represents the time it waits for a message from the Communication Server (PC-3). During this time the other threads with lower priority can run. The *CommunicationManagementTask* still locks the *SlotProcessQueue* shared resource during its wait. This blocks in turn the *TickObserverTask*

---

[3]Time measurements were done by reading the counter value in the RDTSC Pentium register.

Table 10: Analyzed WCRT from Cheddar

Thread	WCRT
IPPacketSendingTask	1322
RLCPDUSendingTask	3047
CommMgtTask	1115
TickObserverTask	4737
DwellReceiverTask	2239

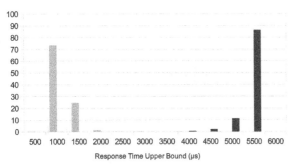

Response Time Upper Bound (µs)

Figure 10: Measured Response Times: Each category represents an interval with the previous category as the lower bound and the current category as the upper bound. Each bar represents the percentage of the corresponding thread's measured response time in the category.

when it wants to access the resource. Since the wait time (equal more or less to the *CommunicationManagementTask*'s 5000µs period) is much greater than the threads' execution time, the *TickObserverTask* takes in average 5000µs to complete. As it cannot finish during the *CommunicationManagementTask*'s wait time, this latter thread is blocked when it wants to access the *NextSlot* shared resource on its next iteration. *TickObserverTask* thus impacts on the *CommunicationManagementTask*'s response time. Blocking a resource for any arbitrary time (e.g. during a thread's inactive time) can not be modeled directly with Cheddar.

We modify the original model in order to verify our assumption on the design mistake.

The modification consists in first applying the lowest priority to the *TickObserverTask*. This is not far from reality since: (1) this thread already has a lower priority than the *IPPacketSendingTask*, (2) *DwellReceiverTask* is always activated before in the scenario we analyze, and (3) *RLCPDUSendingTask* does not have a hard deadline so it is more important for its execution time to reflect on the *TickObserverTask*'s response time.

The second step consists in adding a new thread, called *SleepTask* in the rest of the paper, that is higher in priority than the *TickObserverTask* but lower than the other threads. *SleepTask*'s execution time is computed with the following equation:

$$C(SleepTask) = P(CommMgtTask) - St(SleepTask) \quad (1)$$

Where $C(i)$ is the i thread's capacity, $P(i)$ is i thread's period, $St(i)$ is i thread's release time.

$St(SleepTask)$ is computed as the following:

$$\left(\sum_{x \in h_p(SleepTask)} C(x) \right) + S_{TickObs}(SlotProcessQueue) \quad (2)$$

Where $h_p(i)$ is the set of threads with higher priority than the i thread, and $S_i(r)$ is the time the i thread starts using shared resource r. With the data in table 8 and 9, we get $C(SleepTask) = 952µs$ and $St(SleepTask) = 4048µs$. The *SleepTask* will thus preempt the *TickObserverTask* when it wants to access the *SlotProcessQueue*. The preemption lasts until the *CommunicationManagementTask* is ready to run again, thus simulating the fact that *SlotProcessQueue* is still locked during *CommunicationManagementTask*'s downtime.

The last step of the modification is to change the release time of the *SleepTask* so it preempts the *TickObserverTask* at the exact moment it wants to use the *SlotProcessQueue* shared resource. *TickObserverTask* and *DwellReceiverTask*'s release times have also been changed for more accurate computed WCRT. With this new model it is not possible to apply feasibility tests because of the different release times. We thus do a simulation on a time span of 2 slots, i.e. 10000µs. All threads are still kept periodic to make sure that they have the maximum impact when computing WCRT. Note that the modification only works for computing response times on a time span of 2 slots. *TickObserverTask* will start later in its second activation, having delayed *CommunicationManagementTask*, but *SleepTask*'s release time and capacity cannot be modified. Table 11 shows the computed WCRT from simulation.

Table 11: Simulated WCRT from Cheddar

Thread	WCRT
IPPacketSendingTask	1322
RLCPDUSendingTask	3964
CommMgtTask	3736
TickObserverTask	7619
DwellReceiverTask	2131

By comparing table 11 with the measured response times distribution in figure 10, we see that the results given by simulation, with the more realistic system model, are consistent. This validates our assumption on the design mistake.

The currently suggested MARTE modeling, very near the Cheddar model in its platform design, is limited since an extra modification needed to be done to represent the real system behavior. Furthermore Cheddar's own model is limited as, even with the modification, the simulated behavior only stands true for a limited time span in the case of our experiment.

9.4.2 Missed Deadline

From the simulation by Cheddar, we see that there is at least one case where the *TickObserverTask* misses its 5000µs deadline. This has also been observed in the application's execution, where the thread's maximum observed response time is 5387µs, the average being 5058µs. In reality the system still works because this is a soft deadline. Furthermore not all threads actually run at their WCET, i.e. lateness in certain threads may be compensated by threads running faster in the next slot. The only hard deadline concerns the

CommunicationManagementTask. As long as this thread's response time does not exceed $5000\mu s$, the system works.

We have noticed that there are no feasibility tests implemented in Cheddar for the thread synchronization of our case-study. This justifies the use of the simulator.

9.4.3 Priority Inversion

Another interesting result comes from the Cheddar priority inversion detection tool. Cheddar detects *CommunicationManagementTask* has a priority inversion from 5329 to 7950. 5329 corresponds to the time at which *CommunicationManagementTask* wants to access *NextSlot* and we have:

$$
\begin{aligned}
& C(IPPacketSendingTask) \\
& + C(RLCPDUSendingTask) \\
& + C(TickObs) \\
& - S_{TickObs}(SlotProcessQueue) \\
& = 2621 = 7950 - 5329
\end{aligned} \tag{3}
$$

We remind that in the modified task model we used, *TickObserverTask* has the lowest priority, this is why it is preempted by *RLCPDUSendingTask* too. From the execution traces on the real application, we see that this priority inversion does happen with the *IPPacketSendingTask*. The Gantt chart in figure 11 illustrates this issue. The priority inversion is not surprising as there is no protocol (e.g. PCP, PIP) implemented in un-patched Ubuntu Linux to prevent this phenomenon. The implementation thus need to be deployed on a platform with a real-time OS that supports priority-inversion prevention.

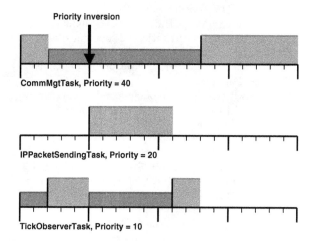

Figure 11: Priority Inversion: A high rectangle means the thread is running, a low rectangle that it is waiting.

9.4.4 Analysis Evaluation Conclusion

In conclusion of our experiment, we can state that we have found a software design mistake in the case-study SRP. The mistake have been detected by comparing analysis results with real measurements. An assumption on the design mistake has been verified with a modified model. With the modified model, the Cheddar schedulability analysis tool gave consistent results. From the results we see that there

is at least one case where a task misses its deadline, a characteristic which has been observed in the execution traces. Finally we also detected that there is at least one case where there is a priority inversion. This phenomenon has also been observed in the execution traces. Such analysis in design phase makes it possible to warn of the importance of priority-inversion prevention mechanisms when choosing a platform for the waveform.

10. CONCLUSION AND FUTURE WORKS

In this paper we have studied the applicability of the real-time scheduling theory on an industrial Software Radio Protocol. We have suggested a solution to apply this theory on a SRP, using a Model-Driven Engineering approach. Our solution uses the UML MARTE profile and the Cheddar schedulability analysis tool. We first analyzed the SRP architecture and its properties for schedulability analysis. Afterwards we defined requirements on the modeling and schedulability analysis. We then modeled the SRP in MARTE and transformed the model to a Cheddar model in order to analyze the system's schedulability. To evaluate the tool's analysis results, we have compared the data with our own measurements on the THALES SRP. We have shown that simulation results from Cheddar are consistent if specific modifications are used to express accurately the system's behavior. The suggested MARTE modeling thus needs to be extended to make it easier for system engineers to express complex thread semantics and interactions.

We plan to work on the following topics in the future. We would like extend the MARTE modeling to include sequence diagrams to describe particular scenarios to analyze. The transformation would then evaluate the diagrams in order to create an accurate Cheddar model.

The tool itself may also need to be extended to express complex semantics and interactions. We have noticed the following lacks in the Cheddar model and the implemented theory: defining an instant for a thread dependency (i.e. the dependent thread does not have to wait for the entire execution of the depended thread), aperiodic burst activation, thread dependency with different periods for dependent and depended, arbitrary time values (e.g. a thread using a shared resource longer than its capacity).

Most SRP developed at THALES are Software Defined Radios (SDR) [21]. These systems are conform to the Software Communications Architecture (SCA) [14]. The SCA adds several mechanisms for interoperability (e.g. middlewares, CORBA [25]) to the platform which make schedulability analysis difficult to do[34]. Implementing the semantics of a software communication bus in Cheddar, and exploring its influence on the analysis results, is part of our future works.

Furthermore the generic task model used in this paper is much too restrictive for analysis of LINK and NET layers. Several works on extending the classical task models have been done [22, 1, 45, 10, 33, 43, 15]. We would like to extend our task model by exploiting the radio channel access protocol's time division nature. By using the time slots allocation, we would like to predict future execution times of tasks instead of using a constant WCET. This is to get less pessimistic analysis results and exploit the prediction for Dynamic Voltage and Frequency Scaling (DVFS) [29] features.

11. ACKNOWLEDGMENTS

This work is performed in the framework of the ARTEMIS funded project PRESTO (http://www.presto-embedded.eu) and FP7 funded project PHARAON. The views expressed in this document do not necessarily represent the views of the complete consortium. The community is not liable for any use that may be made of the information contained herein.

12. REFERENCES

[1] A. Atlas and A. Bestavros. Statistical rate monotonic scheduling. In *Proceedings of the 19th IEEE Real-Time Systems Symposium*, pages 123–132. IEEE Comput. Soc, 1998.

[2] N. Audsley, I. Gray, and S. Indrusiak. Model-based development of embedded systems - the MADES approach. In *Proceedings of the 2nd Workshop on Model Based Engineering for Embedded Systems Design*, 2011.

[3] AUTOSAR. AUTOSAR specification, 2011.

[4] T. S. Chan. Time-Division multiple access. In *Handbook of Computer Networks*, pages 769–778. John Wiley & Sons, Inc., Hoboken, NJ, USA, 2011.

[5] J. A. Davidson. On the architecture of secure software defined radios. In *Proceedings of the 2008 IEEE Military Communications Conference*, pages 1–7. IEEE, 2008.

[6] J. DeAntoni and F. Mallet. TimeSquare: treat your models with logical time. In *Objects, Models, Components, Patterns*, volume 7304, pages 34–41. Springer Berlin Heidelberg, Berlin, Heidelberg, 2012.

[7] V. Debruyne, F. Simonot-Lion, and Y. Trinquet. EAST-ADL - an architecture description language. In *Architecture Description Languages*, volume 176, pages 181–195. Springer-Verlag, New York, 2005.

[8] P. Dissaux and F. Singhoff. Stood and cheddar : AADL as a pivot language for analysing performances of real time architectures. In *Proceedings of the 4th European Congress on Embedded Real Time Software and System*, 2008.

[9] P. H. Feiler, D. P. Gluch, and J. J. Hudak. The architecture analysis & design language (AADL): an introduction. Technical Report ADA455842, Software Engineering Institute, Pittsburgh, 2006.

[10] C. Fotsing, A. Geniet, and G. Vidal-Naquet. A realistic model of Real-Time systems for efficient scheduling. In *Proceedings of the 33rd IEEE Software Engineering Workshop*, pages 3–12. IEEE, 2009.

[11] M. G. Harbour, J. G. Garcia, J. Palencia, and J. Drake Moyano. MAST: modeling and analysis suite for real time applications. In *Proceedings of the 13th Euromicro Conference on Real-Time Systems*, pages 125–134. IEEE Comput. Soc, 2001.

[12] R. Henia, A. Hamann, M. Jersak, R. Racu, K. Richter, and R. Ernst. System level performance analysis - the SymTA/S approach. *IEEE Computers and Digital Techniques*, 152(2):148, 2005.

[13] T. S. Inc. Tri-Pacific software inc. : RAPID RMA. http://www.tripac.com/rapid-rma.

[14] JTRS. Software communication architecture specification, 2012.

[15] L. Ju, A. Roychoudhury, and S. Chakraborty. Schedulability analysis of MSC-based system models. In *Proceedings of the IEEE Real-Time and Embedded Technology and Applications Symposium 2008*, pages 215–224. IEEE, 2008.

[16] K. Klobedanz, C. Kuznik, A. Thuy, and W. Mueller. Timing modeling and analysis for AUTOSAR-based software development: a case study. In *Proceedings of the Conference on Design, Automation and Test in Europe 2010*, 2010.

[17] C. L. Liu and J. W. Layland. Scheduling algorithms for multiprogramming in a Hard-Real-Time environment. *Journal of the ACM*, 20(1):46–61, 1973.

[18] E. Maes and N. Vienne. MARTE to cheddar transformation using ATL. Technical report, THALES Research & Technologies, 2007.

[19] J. Medina and l. G. Cuesta. From composable design models to schedulability analysis with UML and the UML profile for MARTE. In *Proceedings of the 3rd Workshop on Compositional Theory and Technology for Real-Time Embedded Systems*, 2010.

[20] N. Medvidovic and R. Taylor. A classification and comparison framework for software architecture description languages. *IEEE Transactions on Software Engineering*, 26(1):70–93, 2000.

[21] J. Mitola. The software radio architecture. *IEEE Communications Magazine*, 33(5):26–38, 1995.

[22] A. Mok and D. Chen. A multiframe model for real-time tasks. *IEEE Transactions on Software Engineering*, 23(10):635–645, 1997.

[23] OMG. CORBA component model specification, 2006.

[24] OMG. EXPRESS specification, 2010.

[25] OMG. CORBA specification, 2011.

[26] OMG. MARTE specification, 2011.

[27] J. Palencia and M. G. Harbour. Schedulability analysis for tasks with static and dynamic offsets. In *Proceedings of the 19th IEEE Real-Time Systems Symposium*, pages 26–37. IEEE Comput. Soc, 1998.

[28] Papyrus. Papyrus. http://www.eclipse.org/modeling/mdt/papyrus/.

[29] P. Pillai and K. G. Shin. Real-time dynamic voltage scaling for low-power embedded operating systems. *ACM SIGOPS Operating Systems Review*, 35(5):89, 2001.

[30] A. Plantec and F. Singhoff. Refactoring of an ada 95 library with a meta CASE tool. In *Proceedings of the 2006 annual ACM SIGAda international conference on Ada*. ACM Press, 2006.

[31] PrismTech. Spectra CX the SCA development tool. http://www.prismtech.com/spectra/products/spectra-cx.

[32] I. R. Quadri, A. Sadovykh, and L. S. Indrusiak. MADES: a SysML/MARTE high level methodology for real-time and embedded systems. In *Proceedings of the 2012 Embedded Realtime Software and Systems Conference*, 2012.

[33] X. Renault, F. Kordon, and J. Hugues. Adapting models to model checkers, a case study : Analysing AADL using time or colored petri nets. In *Proceedings of the 20th IEEE International Workshop on Rapid System Prototyping*, pages 26–33, Paris, 2009. IEEE.

[34] D. Schmidt. Guest editor's introduction:

Model-Driven engineering. *Computer*, 39(2):25–31, 2006.

[35] S. Sendall and W. Kozaczynski. Model transformation: the heart and soul of model-driven software development. *IEEE Software*, 20(5):42–45, 2003.

[36] L. Sha, T. Abdelzaher, K.-E. Arzen, A. Cervin, T. Baker, A. Burns, G. Buttazzo, M. Caccamo, J. Lehoczky, and A. K. Mok. Real time scheduling theory: A historical perspective. *Real-Time Systems*, 28(2-3):101–155, 2004.

[37] L. Sha, R. Rajkumar, and J. Lehoczky. Priority inheritance protocols: an approach to real-time synchronization. *IEEE Transactions on Computers*, 39(9):1175–1185, 1990.

[38] F. Singhoff, J. Legrand, L. Nana, and L. Marcé. Cheddar: a flexible real time scheduling framework. In *Proceedings of the 2004 Annual ACM SIGAda International Conference on Ada*, pages 1–8. ACM Press, 2004.

[39] F. Singhoff, A. Plantec, P. Dissaux, and J. Legrand. Investigating the usability of real-time scheduling theory with the cheddar project. *Real-Time Systems*, 43(3):259–295, 2009. 10.1007/s11241-009-9072-y.

[40] Smartesting. Smartesting. http://www.smartesting.com/index.php/cms/en/home.

[41] Softeam. Modelio. http://www.modeliosoft.com/.

[42] I. Software. IBM software - rational software architect family. http://www-01.ibm.com/software/awdtools/swarchitect/.

[43] M. Stigge. Schedulability analysis with variable computation time of tasks. Technical report, UPPSALA, 2007.

[44] Symtavision. Symtavision - SymTA/S. http://www.symtavision.com/symtas.html.

[45] N. Tchidjo Moyo, E. Nicollet, F. Lafaye, and C. Moy. On schedulability analysis of non-cyclic generalized multiframe tasks. In *Proceedings of the 2010 22nd Euromicro Conference on Real-Time Systems*, pages 271–278. IEEE, 2010.

[46] THALES. MyCCM. http://sourceforge.net/apps/trac/myccm-hi/wiki.

[47] K. Tindell and J. Clark. Holistic schedulability analysis for distributed hard real-time systems. *Microprocessing and Microprogramming*, 40(2-3):117–134, 1994.

[48] VERDE Consortium. ITEA VERDE. http://www.itea-verde.org/.

[49] VideoLAN. VideoLAN. http://www.videolan.org/vlc/index.html.

[50] H. Zimmermann. OSI reference Model–The ISO model of architecture for open systems interconnection. *IEEE Transactions on Communications*, 28(4):425–432, 1980.

APPENDIX

A. UML DIAGRAMS

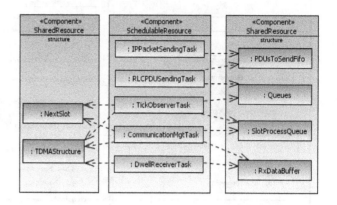

Figure 12: Critical Resource Usage View

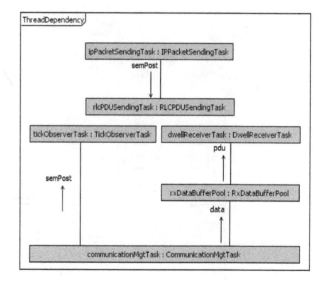

Figure 13: Dependency View

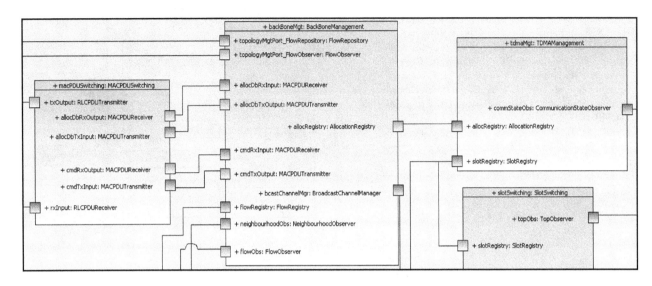

Figure 14: MAC Sub-layer Model

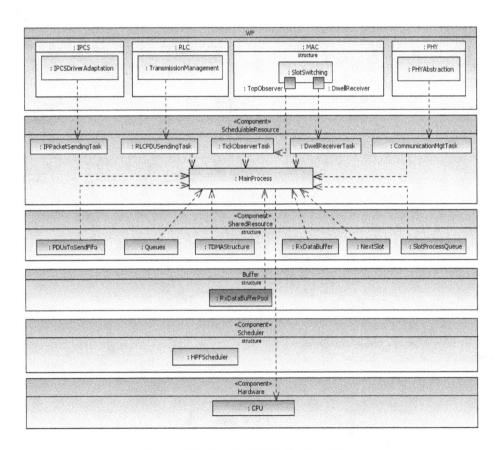

Figure 15: Spatial Distribution View

Programming Language Life Cycles

[keynote presentation]

Guy L. Steele Jr.
Oracle Labs
35 Network Drive UBUR02-313
Burlington, MA 01803
guy.steele@oracle

ABSTRACT

New programming languages keep getting invented, and old languages (most of them) eventually die. Many languages are eventually reduced to, if anything, a single surviving slogan or idea. (Examples: COBOL = programs look like English; SNOBOL = pattern matching on strings.) How do ideas about what programmers want or need to do drive decisions made by language designers? We'll look at some of these ideas, and also at the origin, evolution, and possible destinations of certain ideas pursued during the development of the Fortress programming language, speculating on the forces that drive these life cycles.

Categories and Subject Descriptors

D.3.3 [**Programming Languages**]: Language Constructs and Features

General Terms

Design

Keywords

Ada

Adapting ACATS for use with Run-Time Checks Suppressed

Dan Eilers
Irvine Compiler Corp.
dan@irvine.com

Tero Koskinen
tero.koskinen@iki.fi

ABSTRACT

A well-known issue with compiler conformance testing is that the tested environment may differ from the end user's environment, in ways that defy analysis. Possible differences include the host or target computer instruction set, the host or target computer operating system version, version differences in various components of the compilation system, and differences in compilation switch settings. Most of these differences can be eliminated by retesting in the end-user's actual environment. However, if the end user's environment includes compilation switches that suppress some or all of Ada's run-time checks, which we believe to be quite common, it is not currently feasible to re-run ACATS testing in that mode. That is because many ACATS tests rely on run-time checking, and those tests are not segregated or otherwise identified. We propose to remedy this difficulty by identifying such tests, so that the remaining tests can all be run and expected to pass with compilation flags that suppress some or all checks.

Categories and Subject Descriptors

D.2.4 [**Software Engineering**]: Software/Program Verification—*Validation*; D.3.4 [**Programming Languages**]: Processors—*Compilers*; D.3.2 [**Programming Languages**]: Language Classifications—*Ada*

General Terms

Verification

Keywords

ACATS, run-time, checks, suppressed, conformance, conformance testing, Ada, compiler, Ahven

1. INTRODUCTION

The Ada Conformity Assessment Test Suite (ACATS) [2] is a publicly available test suite intended to check Ada compilers for conformance with the Ada standard [3]. This test suite is useful for many reasons. It helps safety-conscious Ada users avoid errors in Ada compilers; it helps procurement agents avoid incomplete Ada compilers; it helps those who rehost and/or retarget open source Ada compilers to demonstrate successful project completion; it helps compiler vendors perform regression testing; and it helps to promote the viability of Ada providing a comprehensive test of conformance that multiple implementations can be shown to pass.

ACATS, formerly known as ACVC, has been in use for three decades, and has been upgraded extensively, but mostly by means of adding new tests. The framework or organization of the test suite has remained essentially unchanged. Although there remains room for incremental improvement by adding new tests, doing so adds incremental costs and complexity. Instead, we have found room for improvement in the suite's organization, with the goal of improving effectiveness while reducing complexity. Specifically, we note that the ACATS tests are divided into a few main classes, the largest of which is the class of legal executable tests (Class C tests). We propose to subdivide this class into two subclasses, tests that rely on exceptions raised by run-time checks, and those that work correctly even when run-time checks are suppressed.

The main goal of such a subdivision is to substantially improve the effectiveness of ACATS for users who suppress run-time checks. It allows the non-run-time-checking tests to be compiled with some or all checks suppressed, as well as with checks enabled. For users who normally compile their applications with checks suppressed, and wish to test their Ada compiler in the same mode, this would allow them to make use of a substantial well-defined subset of the Class C ACATS tests. Otherwise, the user's confidence in the compiler may unwittingly rely on dubious extrapolation. There is no way to demonstrate simply by analysis that a compiler that behaves correctly when checks are enabled will continue to behave correctly when checks are suppressed, since the paths through the compiler's logic would be different. And in fact we have found some cases where the compiler does behave incorrectly when checks are suppressed.

A secondary benefit of segregating the tests that involve run-time checks is that it may be desirable to have two versions of each of those tests. In one version, the checked values are known statically at compile time. This enables one to see if a compile-time warning is issued, besides ensuring that correct code is generated (where the check itself may be omitted and replaced with an unconditional raise of the exception). In the other version, the checked values are deliberately not knowable at compile time, to ensure that the run-time check has not been omitted.

A third benefit is that collecting all the run-time checking tests together makes it easier to notice any omissions in the checking tests. For example, one might notice that numeric overflow checking is tested for integer types and floating point types, but not for fixed point types, as pointed out in a previous paper [6].

And lastly, we note that currently it can be difficult to determine whether or not a particular combination of language features is tested by ACATS. One may need to search through many test objectives or actual tests. This need arises, for example, when one notices a compiler error and wants to strengthen an existing test, assuming a similar test can be found, in order to prevent such errors in the future. The number of test objectives or actual tests that would need to be examined in order to determine whether or not such a similar test exists would be reduced if the class of executable tests were to be subdivided into two parts, since one generally knows in advance whether the feature combination of interest involves run-time checking.

2. PRIOR WORK

Previously, we have made several other improvements to the framework or organization of ACATS. In particular, we have noted that ACATS does not come with a test harness, nor with automated grading tools. To remedy this, we have integrated ACATS with the AHVEN testing framework, which eliminates the need for OS-specific scripts and other tools to compile, run, and grade the executable tests. This makes ACATS more easily usable by non-experts [5].

We have also noted that ACATS is intended to support grouping multiple executable tests into a single executable program, but this capability doesn't work well for various reasons, particularly including lack of re-initialization of the TCTouch support package. Solutions to these issues are given in the same paper.

We have also noted that nearly 5000 executable test objectives are implemented in the non-executable tests. We have proposed a means of removing the intentional errors from a copy of each of the non-executable tests so that the remaining code, which includes these numerous positive test objectives, can be tested in the context of an executable test. Testing an executable feature in an executable test gives much higher confidence that it is implemented correctly than if it is tested only in a non-executable test [6].

In the course of this prior work, we have uncovered several compiler errors in ACATS-passing implementations by applying the existing ACATS tests in somewhat novel ways. This has encouraged us to continue to find ways to improve the framework or organization of the suite in order to increase its effectiveness at finding errors in compilers, whether they be compile-time failures, or failures in the generated object code.

3. BACKGROUND

One of Ada's benefits is its run-time checking for errors such as buffer overflows and null-pointer dereferences that might otherwise go undetected, with potentially disastrous or at least difficult-to-debug results. But run-time checking is not always wanted or needed, so Ada provides a pragma to suppress it, and compilers typically provide compilation switches to enable the pragma. Anecdotal evidence indicates that many Ada projects take advantage of the ability to suppress some or all run-time checks, at least in selected compilation units.

This may be surprising to some, but each project has its own reasons. The "need for speed" is an obvious reason, particularly in Ada's core market of real-time embedded systems. Such systems often use what might be considered to be underpowered processors, in an attempt to reduce the size, weight, power, cooling, and cost of the processor, or to meet other requirements such as radiation hardening, or to allow headroom for future upgrades.

In some applications, the calculated solution improves with additional computation, such as exploring a search tree of possible moves in an adversarial game, or in monte-carlo simulations. In such cases, checks may be suppressed to maximize the efficiency of the generated code, in order to find the best possible solution, as opposed to simply trying to complete a deterministic calculation before a real-time deadline.

Sometimes code size is a critical factor, particularly in processors with limited address space, or to gain maximum benefit from the instruction cache. So checks may be suppressed to save space.

In some applications, the user can prove that certain runtime checks can never fail, such as elaboration or storage checks. So there is no need to compile with those checks enabled. Sometimes the source code has been proved to be free of all run-time exceptions, perhaps using tools such as SPARK. Similarly, in some applications, the user is confident that testing has demonstrated the program to be sufficiently free of run-time errors to make checks not worthwhile. In other applications, the user may not be particularly concerned about runtime errors corrupting the results of a long computation, because the correctness of the results of the computation can be easily verified.

In some applications, run-time exceptions may be suppressed because they make path-coverage analysis more difficult, particularly when the available test cases do not trigger certain checks, as explained in Section 4.4 of Rosen's paper [4]. Similarly, run-time exceptions may cause exception handling code to appear to be dead code, where coding standards may not allow dead code.

In other applications, hardware error checking, such as for references through null pointers, or floating-point overflow, is considered to be adequate. Software checking may make it easier to locally handle and recover from the exception, but some applications can simply terminate or restart the application when such a fault occurs.

Some Ada users are not particularly affected by the overhead of run-time exceptions, because Ada optimizers can often prove that run-time checks are unnecessary, and optimize them away. But other Ada users do encounter numerous checks in their object code because they choose to disable optimization in order to avoid the possibility of introducing optimization errors or to make the generated code easier to debug or easier to trace back to its source code.

4. MOTIVATION

Test like you fly;
Fly like you test. – *NASA* motto

One might naturally assume that ACATS, being a large and comprehensive test suite, includes tests for all Ada language features, especially those such as Pragma Suppress that have been in the language since the beginning. But a global search using "grep" in the ACATS 3.0 Class C Tests turns up nothing. So we turn to the Ada Compiler Validation Implementers' Guide, which is a document produced along with the initial version of the test suite in 1980 that describes the conditions to be checked by the test suite. It says in Section 11.7: "Since a SUPPRESS pragma need not be obeyed, the only conformity checks we indicate at this time are those needed to check that the pragma is recognized properly. Checks to evaluate whether SUPPRESS is being obeyed will be specified in later versions of the Implementers' Guide." [9]

But our concern isn't whether a Pragma Suppress will be obeyed. Our concern is whether it might trigger a compiler error in code that raises no run-time errors. That isn't something that can be easily tested with a small number of tests, because there's no way of knowing what Ada features might be affected.

Terry Hardy writes: "The failure to test in operational configurations has resulted in a number of system failures and accidents. To the maximum extent possible, tests should replicate actual conditions in operation." [8]

So it is ironic that the most cautious Ada programmer, whose source code has been mathematically proved to be exception free, and whose Ada compiler has been demonstrated to pass all ACATS tests, and who suppresses run-time checks knowing they cannot occur, will be using the compiler in a mode in which ACATS has not been tested at all. We propose to remedy this, by it possible to use ACATS with checks suppressed.

It is not unusual for an Ada compiler to be used differently from the way in which its ACATS testing was performed. The compiler may have been tested running on one version of Linux or Windows, and used on a different version. The compiler may have been tested on an Intel cpu, and used on an AMD cpu. The compiler may have been tested on a 32-bit cpu, and used on a 64-bit cpu. The compiler may have been tested with one level of optimization, and used with a different level of optimization. Some part of the compilation system, especially tools such as a linker that may be supplied by a third party, may have been updated since ACATS testing was performed. Even the compiler itself may be different from what was tested due to intervening maintenance changes.

Such differences defy analysis, but there is a relatively simple solution, as described in the Operating Procedures for Ada Conformity Assessments, Section 7, Extensibility of Conformity Assessment [7]. Just re-run the ACATS tests in the user's actual environment, and compare the results to the original ACATS results. This normally works, except when the difference is that the user is suppressing run-time checks. The reason is that ACATS is intended to be run with all checks enabled, and numerous unspecified tests will not run correctly if checks are suppressed. If we can identify such tests, we can segregate them so that the remaining tests can be run with or without checks suppressed.

5. METHOD

Baptiste Fouques, in an August 2011 posting [1] on the comp.lang.ada newsgroup wrote "I am looking for a referenced list of errors whose detection is required by the Ada Standard." Randy Brukardt replied that "So far as I know, no such list exists. It would be helpful in verifying the coverage (or lack thereof) of the ACATS test suite."

We do have RM 11.5, which specifies Ada's twelve predefined checks, each of which is associated with a predefined exception that is raised when the check fails. Each check can be suppressed or not by using Pragma Suppress or Pragma Unsuppress, and also possibly by compiler flags. Pragma Suppress(All_Checks) can be used to suppress them all. The compiler flag for suppressing all checks is "-gnatp" for Gnat and "-nochecks" for ICC Ada.

The checks and their associated exceptions are:

Access_Check:	Constraint_Error
Discriminant_Check:	Constraint_Error
Division_Check:	Constraint_Error
Index_Check:	Constraint_Error
Length_Check:	Constraint_Error
Overflow_Check:	Constraint_Error
Range_Check:	Constraint_Error
Tag_Check:	Constraint_Error
Accessibility_Check:	Program_Error
Allocation_Check	Program_Error
Elaboration_Check:	Program_Error
Storage_Check:	Storage_Error

But as Randy noted, the Ada RM does not contain a convenient list showing all the circumstances when these run-time checks are applied, nor does the ACATS documentation contain a list showing which run-time checks are tested by which ACATS test. Instead, the run-time checks are scattered throughout the Class C tests.

So our method of finding the ACATS tests that rely on run-time checking is twofold. First we try compiling the executable ACATS tests with checking suppressed, and see which ones fail to execute correctly. This strategy may miss some tests in which compile-time known values allow the compiler to detect that an exception would be raised. In those cases, the compiler might generate code to raise the exception even though checks were suppressed, so the test might run successfully. Secondly we look for compile-time warnings indicating that a run-time exception will invariably be raised, to catch those cases with compile-time known values. An example of such a test is c52104a.

We examine the resulting tests by hand to verify that they indeed involve run-time exceptions, rather than some compiler failure that may have caused them to fail execution with exceptions suppressed.

6. RESULTS

The following table shows the number of tests in each RM chapter that were found to involve run-time checks, meaning they must be compiled with checks enabled to work correctly on all compilers.

Chapter 2	0
Chapter 3	123
Chapter 4	61

6.1 Mixed Tests

We notice that in some of the tests that involve run-time checks, all of the subtests involve run-time checks. But other tests are mixed, with only some subtests involving run-time checks. It may be desirable to eliminate such mixed tests by splitting them into two parts, in order to maximize the number of subtests that can be compiled with checks suppressed.

For example, test c32113a includes 24 subtests, all of which involve run-time checks. But in test c34007d, only 1 of 29 subtests involves run-time checks. The purpose of this test is to verify that the required predefined operations are declared (implicitly) for derived access types whose designated type is a one-dimensional array. Included in this test is a subtest that dereferences a null access value, expecting Constraint_Error to be raised. This subtest is only loosely related to the test's main purpose, and might more appropriately be combined with similar subtests from other tests.

6.2 Defeating Compiler Optimizations

We also notice that the tests involving run-time checks often generate compile-time warnings that a run-time exception will be raised. But some compilers warn on cases that others don't. For example, the last subtest of test c330002 has values being checked that are neither compile-time static, nor protected from data-flow optimization (as is often done using the Ident functions in the Report package).

Although such tests provide an interesting indication of the compile-time optimization capabilities of a compiler, they also indicate where it may be valuable to create additional versions of such subtests, one where the checked values are static (and a warning is expected), and one where the values are protected from compile-time optimization (and a warning is not expected). That way, both paths through each compiler will be exercised.

6.3 Compiler Failures

We found that the use of Pragma Suppress can occasionally cause a compiler to misbehave. For example, one compiler we tested crashed at compile time on test c761010 when checks were suppressed, although this problem has been fixed in later versions. The test involves a record-field initializer that has an allocator with an aggregate bounded by a dynamic function call, as shown in the simplified version below. It would be impractical to develop tests that specifically combine such feature clusters with Pragma Suppress. But such errors can be readily uncovered by applying Pragma Suppress to a large and diverse body of code, such as is found in the ACATS Class C tests.

```
with Text_IO;
procedure P is
    Pragma Suppress(Range_Check);

    function Five return Integer is
    begin
        return 5;
    end Five;

    type String_Ptr is access String;

    type Var_String is
        record
            Comp_1: String_Ptr :=
                new String'(1..Five => 'x');
        end record;

    X1: Var_String;
begin
    Text_IO.Put_Line(X1.Comp_1.all);
end P;
```

7. CONCLUSION

A total of 346 Class C tests were found that must be compiled with run-time checks enabled. The remainder of the Class C tests can be compiled with some or all checks suppressed, providing a substantial new capability for using ACATS in the mode where checks are suppressed.

Acknowledgments.

The authors would like to thank the anonymous referees for their helpful comments.

8. REFERENCES

[1] Baptiste Fouques, "list of errors whose detection is required by RM", comp.lang.ada, August 8, 2011. http://groups.google.com/forum/\#!topic/comp. lang.ada/-5HAYDbXmuI Reprinted in Ada User Journal, Vol 32, No 4 December 2011.

[2] Randall L. Brukardt, "Ada Conformity Assessment Test Suite (ACATS)," http://www.ada-auth.org/acats.html.

[3] S. Tucker Taft, Robert A. Duff, Randall L. Brukardt, Erhard Ploedereder, Pascal Leroy, (Eds.) Ada 2005 Reference Manual. Language and Standard Libraries. International Standard ISO/IEC 8652/1995(E) with Technical Corrigendum 1 and Amendment 1, Lecture Notes in Computer Science, Vol. 4348, Springer, 2006.

[4] J.-P. Rosen, The Ada paradoxes(es), ACM SIGAda Ada Letters, Vol 29, Issue 2, August 2009, pp 28–35.

[5] Dan Eilers and Tero Koskinen, Adapting ACATS to the Ahven Testing Framework. Reliable Software Technologies – Ada-Europe 2011, Lecture Notes in Computer Science, 2011, Vol. 6652/2011, pp. 75–88.

[6] Dan Eilers and Tero Koskinen, Making the non-executable ACATS tests executable. SIGAda 2011, pp. 75–80.

[7] Ada Resource Association, Operating Procedures for Ada Conformity

Assessments, Version 3.0, 2001.
http://www.ada-auth.org/procs/3.0/ACAP30.html

[8] Tery L. Hardy, Software and System Safety:
Accidents, Incidents, and Lessons Learned, 2012; p.
223.

[9] Ada Compiler Validation Implementers' Guide,
SofTech, Inc., Waltham, Massachusetts, October,
1980.

Panel on Compiler Certification

Lennart Beringer
Princeton University
Dept. of Computer Science
35 Olden Street
Princeton, NJ 08540
+1-609-258-0451
eberinge@princeton.edu

Randy Brukardt
Ada Conformity Assessment
Authority
AXE Consultants
621 N. Sherman Ave #B6
Madison WI 53704
+1-608-245-0375
randy@rrsoftware.com

Tom Plum
Plum Hall, Inc.
3 Waihona Box 44610
Kamuela HI 96743 USA
+1- 808-882-1255
tplum@plumhall.com

Moderator:
S. Tucker Taft
AdaCore
24 Muzzey St 3rd Fl
Lexington, MA 02421
+1-781-750-8068 x220
taft@adacore.com

ABSTRACT

Whether programming in a high-level modeling language providing automatic code generation, in a formally-verifiable language, in a language with advanced static analysis tools, or directly in a normal third-generation programming language, we ultimately depend on a *compiler* to generate the actual machine code that is executed by the target machine. This panel will discuss the issue of how we build trust in our compilers, using a commercial test suite, a standardized test suite, or a formal verification process.

Categories and Subject Descriptors

D.2.4 [**Software Engineering**]: Software/Program Verification – *correctness proofs, formal methods, validation*; D.3.4 [**Programming Languages**]: Processors – *compilers.*

Keywords: Compiler validation suite; Formal Verification of Compilers; CompCert; Ada Conformity Assessment

1. INTRODUCTION

Whether programming in a high-level modeling language providing automatic code generation, in a formally-verifiable language, in a language with advanced static analysis tools, or directly in a normal third-generation programming language, we ultimately depend on a *compiler* to generate the actual machine code that is executed by the target machine. This panel will discuss the ways we can build trust in this compiler, given that it is ultimately responsible for generating the executable code derived from our high-integrity programming tools. On our panel we have a founder of the leading vendor of commercial compiler validation suites, the official agent of the authority for assessing the conformity of Ada implementations against the Ada standard, and a member of a team focused on the formal verification of compilers and other development tools.

2. COMMERCIAL TEST SUITE

As long as there have been compilers, there have been compiler test suites. At one time, the National Institute of Standards and Technology provided test suites for various standardized languages, but in the 80's NIST exited the business of developing standard language test suites, and in the 90's NIST stopped performing compiler validations. In the 80's, a market was building for commercial test suites for languages that had not yet reached standardization status. C and C++ in particular attracted the creation of commercial test suites, especially as larger companies became dependent on C and C++ for their business-critical software. Plum Hall was founded in 1979 by Dr. Thomas

Plum and Joan Hall, and began offering a C validation suite in 1986. In fact, C validations performed by NIST and the British Standards Institute were based on commercial test suites, with NIST using one suite, and the BSI using another (Plum Hall, as it turned out). The very first C compiler validation was performed by BSI using the Plum Hall test suite on September 1st, 1990 [1]. Tom Plum will give us the history of his company, and its role in helping to ensure the quality of C, C++, and Java compilers.

3. STANDARDIZED TEST SUITE

A compiler validation suite was planned from the very beginning of the Ada language definition process, which started in the late 70's. This validation suite was called the Ada Compiler Validation Capability (ACVC). The suite was large and thorough, and included both "positive" tests, which were supposed to compile successfully, execute to completion, and print PASSED, and "negative" tests, which were supposed to fail at compile time, because the test violated some legality rule of the language standard. The Ada validation suite grew as the language went through its Ada 95 and Ada 2005 revision, and was renamed in 1998 the Ada Conformity Assessment Test Suite (ACATS) as part of the creation of an ISO standard to define a compiler validation process. Randy Brukardt is the official agent for the Ada Conformity Assesment Authority now responsible for maintaining the ACATS, and will provide insight into the history and ongoing management of the official Ada compiler test suite.

4. FORMAL VERIFICATION

The ultimate certification of a compiler is formal verification. Lennart Beringer is a member of the Verified Software Toolchain project at Princeton University, in cooperation with the formal verification project for the CompCert C compiler at INRIA in France. Lennart will discuss the background and ongoing challenges involved in *proving* that a compiler does exactly what it is supposed to do. The CompCert team described their goal as follows:

> By applying program proof techniques to the source code of the compiler, we can prove, with mathematical certainty, that the executable code produced by the compiler behaves exactly as specified by the semantics of the source~C~program, therefore ruling out all risks of miscompilation.[2].

5. REFERENCES

[1] Jones, D. "C compiler validation is 21 today!", *Shape of Code* blog, 1-Sep-2001, http://shape-of-code.coding-guidelines.com/tag/validation-suite/ (retrieved 10-Oct-2012).

[2] Leroy, X. "CompCert Context and Motivations", http://compcert.inria.fr/motivations.html (retrieved 10-Oct-2012).

Author Index